WAGGY TAILED WISDOM

Lessons in Joy: Bark, Wag, Love!

By Ruby Allure

For Rufus my cheeky little pup who has just blown off under the desk and left me with it. What an inspiration!

Contents

- CHAPTER 1 9
- INTRODUCTION 9
- CHAPTER 2 12
- THE LOVE OF SNIFFIES 12
- CHAPTER 3 15
- A LOVELY BIT OF BARKING 15
- CHAPTER 4 18
- THE JOY OF PLAY: TALES FROM BERTHA THE BICHON FRISE 18
- CHAPTER 5 20
- WHY I LOVE CHASING AND BEING CHASED 20
- CHAPTER 6 23
- THE JOY OF TAIL CHASING 23
- CHAPTER 7 26
- JOHN THE DIPPY DALMATIAN AND THE SHADOW CHASE CHRONICLES 26
- CHAPTER 8 28
- ZOOMIES: A COLLIE'S CHAOTIC ADVENTURE 28
- CHAPTER 9 31
- DOGGY SMILES AND GREETINGS - A POSH POODLE'S PERSPECTIVE 31
- CHAPTER 10 33
- THE ART OF BOTTOM SNIFFING - A CANINE CONVERSATION 33
- CHAPTER 11 36
- THE JOY OF SQUEAKY TOYS - A FRENCH BULLDOG'S FOLLY 36

CHAPTER 12 39
PING PONG'S MIGHTY BARK AND THE ART OF DOOR GUARDING 39
CHAPTER 13 41
THE QUIZZICAL CHARM OF MUPPET'S HEAD TILTS 41
CHAPTER 14 43
PERCY THE PUG'S BOTTOM DRAGGING EXTRAVAGANZA 43
CHAPTER 15 45
RALPH THE ROTTWEILER'S STINK-ROLLING ADVENTURES 45
CHAPTER 16 47
PADDY THE DACHSHUND'S TREAT TEMPTATIONS . 47
CHAPTER 17 49
CRUMPET THE GOLDEN RETRIEVER - THE DINNER TABLE BANDIT 49
CHAPTER 18 51
HARRY THE HUSKY - THE FETCHING EXTRAORDINAIRE 51
CHAPTER 19 53
TERRY THE BOXER - THE SLOBBER MAESTRO 53
CHAPTER 20 55
BOB THE BASSET HOUND - SOCK ENTHUSIAST EXTRAORDINAIRE 55
CHAPTER 21 57
SHEILA THE SHIH TZU - THE MASTER OF PUPPY MISCHIEF 57
CHAPTER 22 59

MIKE THE MASTIFF – THE WHIZZ OF RANDOM CHEWS 59

CHAPTER 23 61

RUBY THE POINTER - THE DIGGER AND HIDER EXTRAORDINAIRE 61

CHAPTER 24 63

THE MALTESE MARVEL - A LAP DOG'S GUIDE TO AFFECTION 63

CHAPTER 25 65

COLIN THE CAVAPOO - THE MASTER OF HILARIOUS SNEEZES 65

CHAPTER 26 67

DELILA THE GREAT DANE - QUEEN OF FURNITURE STEALING 67

CHAPTER 27 69

GLORIA THE GREYHOUND - IN PURSUIT OF THE INVISIBLE 69

CHAPTER 28 71

PERRY THE PEKINGESE - THE ART OF GIFT-GIVING 71

CHAPTER 29 73

SPROUT THE YORKSHIRE TERRIER - CHASING THE ELUSIVE REFLECTION 73

CHAPTER 30 75

BETTY THE BLOODHOUND - WIND IN MY FUR AND A BIG DOGGY SMILE 75

CHAPTER 31 77

BRENDA THE BOLOGNESE - THE ART OF TOY THEFT 77

CHAPTER 32	79
DARRYL THE DREVER - THRIVING IN A PACK	79
CHAPTER 33	82
RUFUS'S WISDOM - THE ART OF THE "TUM TUM"	82
CHAPTER 34	85
JEFF'S DREAMLAND ADVENTURES	85
THE ART OF RUNNING IN THEIR SLEEP	85
CHAPTER 35	88
JASPER'S DOORWAY DILEMMAS - THE MYSTERY OF AUTOMATIC DOORS	88
CHAPTER 36	90
CANDICE'S CURIOUS CHRONICLES - THE ART OF CROTCH SNIFFING	90
CHAPTER 37	92
ALF'S LICK-TASTIC ADVENTURES - SELF-GROOMING SHENANIGANS	92
CHAPTER 38	94
TREAT AND GREET - A WEIMARANER'S PERSPECTIVE	94
CHAPTER 39	97
THE PLAYFUL "DOGGY CONGA" - A BULL TERRIER'S PERSPECTIVE	97
CHAPTER 40	99
BATHROOM BUDDIES: A VIZSLA'S PERSPECTIVE	99
CHAPTER 41	101
TOILET TIDBITS: A SHAPENDOS'S PERSPECTIVE	101
CHAPTER 42	103

MUDDY MARVELS: A MUDI'S PERSPECTIVE 103

CHAPTER 43 105

AVOIDING THE BATH AND EMBRACING THE POST-BATH ZOOMIES 105

CHAPTER 44 107

THE SHAKE - A DOG'S RESET BUTTON 107

CHAPTER 45 109

LOIS, THE LHASA APSO'S LICKING ADVENTURES . 109

CHAPTER 46 111

FETCHING FUN WITH CYRIL THE IRISH WOLFHOUND 111

CHAPTER 47 114

SQUIRREL-CHASING ADVENTURES WITH BOWIE THE SAUSAGE DOG 114

CHAPTER 48 117

WALKIES WONDERLAND - A WOLFHOUND'S TALE 117

CHAPTER 49 119

STARING AT MY HUMANS - A DOG'S JEDI MIND TRICK 119

CHAPTER 50 122

THE ENCHANTING WORLD OF DEERS AND RABBITS - SOFIA'S PERSPECTIVE 122

CHAPTER 51 125

THE TWIRL BEFORE THE POOP - HARRY'S TALES 125

CHAPTER 52 128

GAS AND GIGGLES - GEMIMA'S PERSPECTIVE 128

CHAPTER 53 130

THE ART OF WAGGING - TALES OF A LABRADOR'S TAIL 130

CHAPTER 54 132

THE JOY OF HOWLING: A LAPPONIAN HERDER'S PERSPECTIVE 132

CHAPTER 55 134

CANINE CULINARY CAPERS - A SALUKI'S PERSPECTIVE 134

CHAPTER 56 136

SNOOZING IN UNUSUAL POSITIONS - A DOG'S PERSPECTIVE 136

CHAPTER 57 138

DOGGY KISSES AND NUZZLES - A LOVE LANGUAGE BY MISSY THE AKITA 138

CHAPTER 58 140

BEING A GOOD BOY AND A GOOD GIRL - LESSONS IN PRAISE AND JOY 140

CHAPTER 59 143

UNCONDITIONAL LOVE - A TERRIER'S PERSPECTIVE 143

CHAPTER 60 146

DOGGY DIVAS AND MASTER MANIPULATORS - A CANINE PERSPECTIVE 146

CHAPTER 61 148

THE BEST THINGS ABOUT BEING A DOG 148

CHAPTER 1

INTRODUCTION

Woof, woof! Howl-dy, dear humans, and welcome to *Waggy Tailed Wisdom - Lessons in Joy: Bark, Wag, Love!* I'm Rufus, your four-legged guide to the delightful world of doggy insights, and my tail is wagging furiously with excitement to share our tales with you.

In this enchanting collection, you'll embark on a paw-some journey through the eyes of some of my fellow canine companions. We'll unravel the mysteries of the tail-wagging art, explore the joyous wonders of the world, and uncover the secrets of spreading love and laughter. But before we dive into the stories, let me give you a sneak "pupdates" on what you'll discover within these virtual pages:

Hilarious Hijinks: From chasing our own shadows to barking at inanimate objects, we dogs have quite the talent for turning everyday situations into uproarious adventures. Get ready for some tail-wagging humour!

Lessons in Love: You'll witness the heart-warming tales of unconditional love and affection, from cuddles to head tilts. Dogs like me have mastered the art of spreading love to brighten your day.

Paw-spective: Ever wondered what's going on in that furry head of ours? We'll provide insights into our quirky behaviours and why we do the things we do. Get ready to see life from a new "paw-spective."

Waggy Tailed Wisdom: In each tale, you'll find nuggets of wisdom inspired by our doggy adventures. These lessons are here to remind you of the simple joys of life, the importance of love and laughter, and how to embrace every moment with a wagging tail.

So, fasten your seatbelts (or should I say, leash up your curiosity), and let's embark on this delightful journey together. Whether you're a lifelong dog lover or just starting to discover the wonders of the canine world, there's something for everyone in "Waggy Tailed Wisdom." Prepare to bark, wag, and love your way through these enchanting tales!

Are you ready? Let's unleash the wisdom and share the joy. Tail wags and nose bops to you all!

WOOF! WOOF!

Love Rufus, (Ruby's pup)

BE MORE DOG

I am a dog, and I love life because,
I chase the wind, I chase my dreams, I never pause.
With tail a-wagging, and heart so free,
In each moment's joy, I find the key.

Through fields I run, in the sun's warm embrace,
A world of wonders, a smile on my face.
No worries of tomorrow, no sorrows of the past,
In the present moment, my happiness will last.

So let us all remember, both woman and man,
To cherish life's moments, just as I can.
With love and laughter, and a heart that's agog,
Embrace each new day with the motto: "Time to be more dog!"

CHAPTER 2

THE LOVE OF SNIFFIES

Dear Human,

I wish I could talk your language, but since I can't, I'll do my best to share my thoughts through these wagging paws and hopeful eyes. You see, every time we go on one of our wonderful walks, I experience a world that's beyond words, and I want to tell you all about it.

When we venture to the sea, the first thing that captivates me is the air—the crisp, salty air that tingles my nose and fills my heart with excitement. I can sense the vastness of the ocean, stretching out as far as my keen eyes can see. Each wave brings stories of far-off places, adventures, and mysteries. It's as if the sea is whispering secrets, and I'm the lucky one who gets to listen.

Then we visit the park, and that's where the real fun begins. Every blade of grass, every tree, and even the benches and lampposts are like bulletin boards covered in 'pee-mail.' You might not notice, but my nose is a detective, and it's always working overtime. I can tell who's been here, whether they were happy or curious, and sometimes, I even get tips on where the best squirrel chases are happening. It's a whole world of canine communication, and I'm fluent in it.

But the grand finale is our trips to the forest. The moment we step in, it's as if I'm entering a different realm. The earthy, woody scent that surrounds me is like a symphony playing just for me. Each tree, each leaf, and every nook and cranny hold a story. I follow the scents of rabbits, squirrels, and birds, imagining their adventures and escapades. It's a magical place where I feel truly connected to the wild at heart.

But here's what I've come to realise on our walks: life is not just about going from one place to another or rushing to the next task. It's about savouring the moments, relishing the details, and embracing the joy of discovery. The 'sniffies' I enjoy on our walks aren't just about the smells; they're about the stories and connections they bring.

So, my dear human, as much as I'd love to share these experiences with you in words, all I can do is encourage you to slow down, be present, and cherish the 'sniffies' of your own life. Just as I find delight in each scent, you can find pleasure in the small, often unnoticed moments. Let your senses guide you, and you'll uncover a world of joy waiting to be savoured.

With every tail wag and nudge, I hope you understand that I'm telling you how wonderful it is to explore the world together, one 'sniffy' at a time. Thank you for being my partner on this incredible journey.

Yours in joyful exploration,

Mable

CHAPTER 3

A LOVELY BIT OF BARKING

Oh, hello there! I'm Sinbad, an intact male Schnauzer, and I've got something quite important to tell you about: barking. You see, barking isn't just noise for us dogs; it's an art, a form of expression, and oh, what a pleasure it can be.

First, let me introduce you to the dogs I encounter in my daily adventures. There's Max, the neighbour's Golden Retriever. Max is a friendly fellow, and my barks to him are like a hearty greeting. It's my way of saying, "Hey there, pal, how's your day going?" Max responds with his own joyful woofs, and together, we create a harmonious chorus of happiness.

Then, there's Bella, the mischievous Beagle who lives down the street. Bella and I engage in what you might call a "barking conversation." It's like a game of call and response. I bark; she barks back. It's a delightful back-and-forth, a bit of banter that keeps our tails wagging.

Now, let's not forget about Mr. Whiskers, the neighbourhood cat who thinks he owns the place. Whenever Mr. Whiskers dares to cross my path, I give him my fiercest bark, asserting my territory. He may not understand my words, but he gets the message loud and clear: "This is Schnauzer turf!" It's a satisfying bark of authority, you see.

And then there's the postman, Mr. Johnson. Oh, he's a good sport. My barks at him are like a daily ritual, a friendly reminder that he's welcome here, but I must ensure he doesn't forget. It's a responsible bark, one that keeps our mail deliveries running smoothly.

But let me tell you about the types of barks. There's the excited bark when I see my leash, signalling the joy of our impending walk. There's the playful bark when I spot a squirrel up a tree, inviting it to join in the chase. And then there's the alert bark when I sense something amiss, like a stranger approaching. Each bark has its own flavour, its own purpose, and it's pure bliss to let them out.

Now, for the 'Waggy Tailed Wisdom' I'd like to share with you, dear humans. Barking isn't just about making noise; it's about expressing ourselves and connecting with the world around us. So, my advice to you is this: find your own form of barking. It could be singing in the shower, dancing in the rain, or even laughing with friends. Let it be your way of saying, "I'm here, I'm alive, and I'm joyful."

Embrace the different types of 'barks' in your life, whether they're moments of excitement, playfulness, or alertness. Use them to connect with others, assert your presence, and express your emotions. Just as I find pleasure in my barks, you can find joy in being yourself and sharing your unique voice with the world.

So, dear humans, go ahead and let out a lovely bit of barking in your own way. I promise you'll find that life becomes a whole lot more enjoyable when you do.

With barks of happiness,

Sinbad

CHAPTER 4

THE JOY OF PLAY: TALES FROM BERTHA THE BICHON FRISE

Hey there, humans and furry friends! I'm Bertha, the Bichon Frise, and I'm here to share with you the sheer delight and wonder of playtime. You see, in the world of dogs, play isn't just a simple activity—it's a way of life, a language, and a boundless source of happiness.

Let's talk about that magical moment when playtime begins. It's all about the paw tap—a gentle, friendly gesture that says, "Hey, let's have some fun!" With one little tap of my paw, I can ignite a whirlwind of excitement. It's like starting a party where everyone's invited, and the more, the merrier!

I've got an impressive repertoire of play moves, from the classic "chase me" sprint to the graceful "catch the tail" twirl. My zoomies around the yard can rival a Formula 1 race, and my leaps can reach heights that even humans envy. I'm a master of the sneak attack, pouncing from behind a couch or darting out from a hiding spot to surprise my pals.

But the best part of play isn't the acrobatics or the games we play—it's the pure, unadulterated joy we share. It's the laughter in our barks, the wagging of our tails, and the sparkle in our eyes. It's the way we forget our worries and embrace the present moment.

Now, let's talk about getting others to play. You see, I'm quite the persuasive pup. When I want someone to join in the fun, I turn on the charm. I'll nuzzle, nudge, and use my best puppy-dog eyes until they can't resist. And guess what? It usually works like a charm. Because who can resist the invitation to play?

As for waggy tailed wisdom, here's what I have to share: Embrace play with open arms, whether you're a dog or a human. Play isn't just for puppies; it's for everyone, no matter their age. It's a reminder that life is meant to be filled with laughter, connection, and moments of unbridled joy.

So, my dear friends, don't forget to indulge in the simple pleasure of play. Whether it's a game of fetch, a romp in the park, or a friendly paw tap to initiate a game, cherish those moments of shared happiness. For in play, we find a beautiful expression of love, companionship, and the true essence of living in the moment.

With a wag and a woof,

Bertha

CHAPTER 5

WHY I LOVE CHASING AND BEING CHASED

Hi there, I'm Fidget, a Whippet with a need for speed! You might wonder why I'm so obsessed with chasing and being chased, so let me tell you—it's an endless source of joy, excitement, and connection in my world.

First, let's talk about the different chases I enjoy. There's the classic game of fetch, where a ball or a frisbee takes flight, and I spring into action. The thrill of chasing that object, feeling the wind in my fur, and the sheer exhilaration of the catch—it's like a symphony of delight for me. Each leap and bound is a small victory, a reminder of the simple pleasure of movement.

Then there are the squirrel chases. Those fluffy-tailed creatures have an uncanny ability to dart up trees just when I think I have them cornered. It's a game of strategy and quick reflexes, and even if I don't catch them, the chase itself is a heart-pounding adventure.

But the most special chases are the ones I share with my fellow four-legged friends. When I see a buddy at the park or on the beach, there's an unspoken agreement: we're in for a good chase. The joy of running side by side, taking turns being the chaser and the chased—it's a dance of camaraderie and laughter. These chases are like a language of their own, a way of saying, "I see you, I'm with you, and we're in this together."

Now, let's talk about being chased. Oh, what a thrill it is when someone decides to chase me! Whether it's a game of tag with a friend or a human playfully chasing me around the yard, being pursued ignites a fire of excitement within me. It's like a reminder that I'm loved, valued, and wanted—a feeling I wish every being could experience.

You know, the 'Waggy Tailed Wisdom' I'd like to share with you humans is simple but profound: Embrace the joy of chase in your own lives. Find those moments of excitement, movement, and connection. Maybe it's a friendly game of tag with your loved ones, a spontaneous dance, or a pursuit of your passions and dreams.

Just as I find happiness in the thrill of the chase, you can discover pleasure in pursuing the things that make your heart race with excitement. And don't forget to cherish the moments when you're pursued, too, because being wanted and loved is a precious gift.

So, my dear humans, go ahead and chase your dreams, chase your happiness, and chase each other with open hearts. In the pursuit, you'll find the true essence of joy and connection.

With a racing heart and a wagging tail,

Fidget

CHAPTER 6

THE JOY OF TAIL CHASING

Hi there, I'm Doughnut, the Springer Spaniel with a never-ending supply of enthusiasm and an undying love for tail chasing. You might call me a bit 'dappy,' but I like to think of it as having an extra helping of zest for life.

Let me tell you, there's nothing quite like the thrill of chasing one's own tail. The moment I spot it, that fuzzy, curly thing right behind me, I can't resist the urge to give it a whirl. I leap into action, spinning in circles with unbridled enthusiasm. Round and round I go, my eyes locked on that elusive target.

Now, you might wonder, "Why chase your own tail, Doughnut?" Well, my dear human friends, there's something utterly magical about it. As I spin, I can feel the world around me blur into a whirl of colours and sensations. It's like a merry-go-round ride right in my own backyard. The dizziness, the giddiness—it's like a burst of laughter that bubbles up from deep within me.

And let me tell you, there's no better way to shake off the cobwebs and embrace the pure joy of the present moment. I'm not thinking about yesterday or worrying about tomorrow—I'm fully immersed in the here and now, chasing my tail with all my might.

Of course, my tail-chasing escapades often lead to some rather comical situations. You see, I get so engrossed in the chase that I forget about things like furniture, walls, and even other pets. I've been known to bump into things, tumble over my own paws, and, on occasion, collide with the unsuspecting cat. But you know what? It's all part of the fun! Life's a bit like a slapstick comedy when you're a tail-chasing Springer.

Now, let's talk about the 'Waggy Tailed Wisdom' I have to offer. My tail-chasing antics remind us humans to find joy in the simplest of activities. Whether it's dancing in the rain, singing in the shower, or laughing until your sides hurt, don't be afraid to embrace your inner goofiness. Take a moment to let loose, be present, and savour the sheer joy of the moment.

Just as I find delight in chasing my tail, you can find pleasure in being a little 'dappy' and spontaneous from time to time. Life doesn't always have to be serious business, and sometimes, the best moments are the ones where you let go and just have fun.

So, my dear humans, remember to chase your own tail of happiness, and let the giddiness of the moment sweep you off your feet. After all, life's too short not to indulge in a little silliness.

With a wagging tail and a twirl,

Doughnut

CHAPTER 7

JOHN THE DIPPY DALMATIAN AND THE SHADOW CHASE CHRONICLES

Halloa, humans! I'm John, a Dalmatian with a name as unique as my personality. You may be wondering how I ended up with the rather human name of John. Well, it's a tale as peculiar as my penchant for chasing my own shadow.

You see, when I was just a pup, I had a bit of a reputation for being, well, dippy. My owner, a wise old soul, took one look at my spots and my boundless enthusiasm for chasing my own tail, and he decided that a simple, classic name like John would be the perfect fit.

But let's talk about my favourite pastime - chasing my own shadow. It's a delightful game of "chase" that I engage in whenever the sun casts my shadow just right. The shadow darts and dances, mimicking my every move, and I, in my dappy glory, am convinced that I'm pursuing the sneakiest critter in town.

I leap and twirl, my paws stomping the ground in wild anticipation, as I chase that elusive shadow. It's a game that never grows old, and each time feels like the very first. Oh, the laughter it brings to my owner and anyone lucky enough to witness my antics.

Now, for the 'Waggy Tailed Wisdom' I'd like to impart. Shadows may seem like mere illusions, but they hold profound insights. In your world, shadows represent the parts of yourself that you may not always fully understand or accept.

Just as I chase my shadow with boundless enthusiasm, I encourage you to confront your own shadows with curiosity and an open heart. Embrace the quirks and imperfections that make you unique. Behind the dappyness of life, there lies a wealth of wisdom and insight waiting to be discovered.

So, dear humans, let your inner John shine through. Chase your shadows of doubt, fear, or uncertainty, and in doing so, you'll uncover the hidden gems of your true self. Embrace the laughter, the quirks, and the wisdom that life offers, even in the most unexpected places.

With a dappy dance and a heart full of wisdom,

John

CHAPTER 8

ZOOMIES: A COLLIE'S CHAOTIC ADVENTURE

Hello there, I'm Sky, the Collie with boundless energy and a penchant for the perplexing phenomenon known as "Zoomies." You might say I'm a picture of elegance most of the time, but when the Zoomies strike, all bets are off!

Zoomies, my dear humans, are those moments when an irresistible surge of energy courses through my veins, and I simply must run like a maniac, even if there's no apparent reason. It's like a tidal wave of excitement crashing upon the shores of my soul. And let me tell you, it's an adventure like no other.

The Zoomies often catch me off guard. One moment, I'm peacefully lounging, and the next, I'm on my paws, tongue flailing, and eyes wide with exhilaration. There's no rhyme or reason to it, but oh, the joy it brings!

As I zoom through the house, I have a tendency to leap over things with the grace of a gymnast in the Olympics. Beds become trampolines, the sofa transforms into a launching pad, and even the coffee table is fair game for my aerial acrobatics. I imagine myself as a fearless daredevil soaring through the skies, my fur trailing behind me like a majestic cape.

But here's the funny part, my Zoomies often land me in the most peculiar situations. I've been known to accidentally launch myself into the laundry basket, and once, I got stuck under the dining room table. But you know what? I don't mind a bit of chaos—it's all part of the Zoomies experience!

Now, let's talk about the 'Waggy Tailed Wisdom' I'd like to share. The Zoomies remind us humans that sometimes, it's perfectly okay to embrace moments of spontaneity and let your inner child run wild. Life can be so serious, but it doesn't always have to be.

So, whether it's dancing like nobody's watching, singing in the shower at the top of your lungs, or simply laughing until your belly hurts, don't hold back. Let your inner Zoomie out to play, and don't worry about where you land. The journey is what matters most.

Just as I find joy in my frenetic bursts of energy, you can find pleasure in letting go, feeling giddy, and embracing the unexpected. Life is an adventure, and sometimes, the best moments are the ones where you leap without looking.

So, my dear humans, don't be afraid to embrace your inner Sky and go on a Zoomies adventure of your own. After all, a little chaos can be a whole lot of fun!

With a bound and a bouncy heart,

Sky

CHAPTER 9

DOGGY SMILES AND GREETINGS - A POSH POODLE'S PERSPECTIVE

Greetings, darling humans! I'm Porsha, the epitome of poise and sophistication, or so I like to think. You see, in the world of doggy smiles and greetings, I have quite the flair for the dramatic.

First, let's talk about the circling. Oh, the circling! When I approach a fellow canine or even a human companion, I like to make a grand entrance. I gracefully glide in a circle, my fluffy tail held high, as if I were twirling in a ballroom dance. It's all part of my regal charm, you see, and I wouldn't have it any other way.

Now, let's move on to the sniffing and nudging of ears. When it comes to greetings, I believe in the art of subtlety. I delicately approach, my nose in the air, and take in the exquisite scents around me. A gentle nudge of the ear or a dainty sniff here and there, and I've exchanged pleasantries without a hair out of place. It's all about leaving an impression of grace and elegance.

But here's where the humour comes in. Sometimes, in my enthusiasm to be the perfect hostess or guest, I forget myself. I get so carried away in my greetings that I've been known to knock over a tea set or accidentally step on a fellow dog's tail. Oh, the scandal! It's a reminder that even the poshest of Poodles can have their moments of clumsiness.

Now, let's discuss the 'Waggy Tailed Wisdom' I'd like to impart. Doggy smiles and greetings are all about making connections and spreading joy. It's a lesson for humans, too. In your interactions with others, whether they're friends, family, or even strangers, take a moment to greet them with warmth and sincerity.

A smile, a friendly hello, or a kind gesture can go a long way in brightening someone's day. And don't be afraid to let your authentic self shine through, even if it means a little awkwardness now and then. After all, life is meant to be lived with a dash of humour and a whole lot of heart.

So, my dear humans, channel your inner Porsha and approach each day with grace, charm, and a generous dose of kindness. And remember, a warm greeting and a genuine smile can make the world a more delightful place.

With a twirl and a curtsy,

Porsha

CHAPTER 10

THE ART OF BOTTOM SNIFFING - A CANINE CONVERSATION

Hello, darling humans! I'm Chuck the Chua Wawa, and this is Daisy, she is an old English sheep dog. We'd like to regale you with tales of the refined art of bottom sniffing, as seen through our canine eyes.

"That's right, Chuck," said Daisy, panting, her hair arranged in a ponytail above her eyes so she could see. "We may be different breeds, but we share a mutual appreciation for this sophisticated practice, and we both have slightly different challenges..."

Daisy glanced at Chuck, and then her bottom itched, so she dragged her bottom across the floor with her tongue flaying.

'Indeed, Daisy' said Chuck with a chuckle, "Bottom sniffing, though elegant, has its fair share of complexities, doesn't it?"

Daisy nodded in her special doggy way. "Absolutely, Chuck. You smaller dogs often face bottoms at face level, like trying to reach the top shelf in a kitchen. You must employ the art of standing on hind legs with grace and elegance".

Chuck sighed in agreement, "So woofing true, Daisy. And for larger dogs like you, their bottoms are like mountains, and you must scale them with finesse. It's like conquering Everest daily. Whereas it must be a challenge for you when having to descend to the lower posterioral levels of smaller pups.

Daisy made a doggy chortle "Oh, Chuck, you're quite the wordsmith. And what about those magnificent tails? Finding the bottom amidst all that fluff is like searching for a needle in a haystack or a bone in a field.

Chuck made a special doggy grin of agreement. "Our pursuit can sometimes lead to hilarious mishaps. Bottom sniffing is not for the faint of heart.

Daisy responded with a flourish as she reminisced over all the bottoms she had stiffed. "So, to all you lovely humans how can we inspire you with bottom sniffing? Well, how about you embrace the diversity of life because not every bottom smells the same. Find joy in the quirks and idiosyncrasies of your fellow beings. Just as we find delight in bottom sniffing, you can find it in connecting with one another on a deeper level and you don't even have to sniff them.

Chuck remained thoughtful. "There is also aspiration to consider which can be comparable to a good bottom sniff. One may have to jump to align with bottoms at a higher level or make special efforts to attain a bottom that may be out of reach. How does that apply to waggy tailed wisdom? Well, where there is a will there is a bottom sniffing way… In the meantime, here's to the art of bottom sniffing and to understanding and connection among humans!" Chuck said raising a tiny paw

"Cheers, my dear friends! I hope this explains a few things…" said Daisy as she nuzzled Chuck

Love

Chuck and Daisy

CHAPTER 11

THE JOY OF SQUEAKY TOYS - A FRENCH BULLDOG'S FOLLY

Hello, delightful humans! I'm Georgia, the French Bulldog, and I have a confession to make - I have an unbridled passion for squeaky toys. Those little marvels of noise and mirth that bring so much joy to my life.

But oh, the chaos they can unleash! You see, squeaky toys have this incredible power to scare the heck out of my dear owner. Picture this: I'm in the living room, minding my own business, when I suddenly pounce on my squeaky toy with all my might. Squeak! The noise reverberates through the house, and my owner jumps out of their skin, thinking there's some strange creature in the room.

And it's not just random moments. Oh no! I have an impeccable sense of timing. I love to seize my squeaky toy when my owner is on an important phone call or trying to concentrate on work. Squeak! Their startled expressions are priceless, really.

But it's not all about mischief. The joy of the squeak itself is indescribable. I'll spend hours just squeezing that little thing between my teeth, my eyes wide with delight. Squeak! It's music to my ears.

Now, let me share a tale of my cheekiness. You see, I have this habit of sneaking into my owner's bed and hiding squeaky toys under their pillows. It's my way of saying, "Surprise! Sweet dreams." Of course, it often catches my owner off guard when they find squeaky treasures in the most unexpected places.

Then there was that one time when my owner made the mistake of taking my squeaky toy away from me while driving. Well, let's just say I couldn't let that stand. I unleashed a chorus of squeaks that had my owner desperately trying to reverse the car amidst the symphony of sound. It was quite the adventure!

And oh, the night-time escapades. When nature calls in the middle of the night, I decide it's the perfect time to grab my squeaky toy. Why? Because I can! The darkness, the silence, and then, SQUEAK! My owner's sleep-deprived expression is a sight to behold.

Now, for the 'Waggy Tailed Wisdom' I'd like to share with humans. The joy of a squeaky toy is not to be underestimated. In our playfulness, we remind you to find delight in the simple things in life. Embrace the unexpected moments of laughter, even if they startle you or disrupt your routine.

And maybe, just maybe, you can use the element of surprise to add a dash of humour to your life. Like when you set up a squeaky toy for your unsuspecting friend to step on, and you both burst into laughter at their reaction. It's these moments of shared amusement that make life all the more wonderful.

As for me, I'll continue my squeaky adventures, dodging and darting with my prised possession, leading my owner on merry chases, and sharing laughter in the most unexpected ways. After all, life is better with a little squeak and a lot of fun!

With a mischievous bark and a joyful squeak,

Georgia

CHAPTER 12

PING PONG'S MIGHTY BARK AND THE ART OF DOOR GUARDING

Howdy doody, dear humans! I'm Ping Pong, a Pomeranian pup with a bark that belies my tiny stature. You see, I have a very important job - guarding the door. And I take this duty very, very seriously.

First, let's address the obvious - I may be small, fluffy, and undeniably cute, but don't let that fool you. I am convinced that I possess the mightiest bark in the canine kingdom. It's a bark that echoes through the ages, a bark that strikes fear into the hearts of postal workers and passers-by alike.

Every day, I stand vigilant by the door, my fluffy tail held high like a flag of warning. The moment I hear the gentle creak of the mailbox or the approaching footsteps of the postman, I unleash my bark, loud and proud. It's a symphony of tiny fury, a burst of sound that reverberates through the neighbourhood.

And the reactions, oh, they're priceless. The postman jumps as if he's just seen a ghost, and the passers-by exchange knowing glances, their faces a mixture of amusement and surprise. You see, dear humans, I've mastered the art of the "cute surprise."

But there's more to it than just startling unsuspecting souls. I'm a firm believer in protecting my territory, no matter how small it may be. The door is my castle, and I am its brave guardian. It's an instinct that runs deep within me, a need to ensure that my home is safe and sound.

Now, for the 'Waggy Tailed Wisdom' I'd like to share with you. Barking at the door isn't just about making noise; it's about standing up for what's important to you. In your world, find your own "door" to guard. It could be your dreams, your loved ones, or even your beliefs.

And don't underestimate the power of being cute and fluffy. Sometimes, the most unassuming individuals can make the biggest impact. Just as I take pride in my tiny yet mighty bark, you can find strength in your unique qualities.

So, dear humans, let your inner Ping Pong shine through. Stand tall, or in my case, stand small but fierce, and protect what matters most to you. Embrace the element of surprise and take pride in your own "mighty bark." After all, it's the little things that can make the biggest difference.

With a brave bark and a fluffy tail,

Ping Pong

CHAPTER 13

THE QUIZZICAL CHARM OF MUPPET'S HEAD TILTS

Hello, lovely humans! I'm Muppet, a Lady King Charles Spaniel with a penchant for the most adorable head tilts you've ever seen. Now, let me take you on a journey through the delightful world of my head tilting escapades.

First, let's address the "why" behind my head tilting. You see, dear humans, it's all about curiosity. When you ask me a question or make a strange noise, my world transforms into a puzzle waiting to be solved. I simply can't resist the urge to tilt my head to the side, as if to say, "Tell me more, please!"

For instance, when my owner lets out a peculiar noise, like passing wind, I am utterly baffled. The source of the sound remains a mystery to me. I tilt my head to the left, then to the right, and sometimes even give it a little shake, hoping to unravel the enigma of the phantom noise.

But it's not just unusual sounds that trigger my head tilts. When my owner holds up a treat and asks if I want it, my head tilts in excitement. Of course, I want it! I practically do somersaults of joy while maintaining my charming head tilt.

And when my tiny human companion babbles away in their adorable baby talk, I tilt my head in fascination, as if trying to decipher the secret language of the little one. It's like having a front-row seat to a never-ending comedy show.

Now, for the 'Waggy Tailed Wisdom' I'd like to share with you. The joy of head tilting is all about embracing life's mysteries and finding humour in the everyday moments. In your world, take a lesson from my quirks.

When faced with something puzzling or unexpected, don't be afraid to tilt your own metaphorical "head" and explore it with an open heart. Life is full of delightful surprises and funny moments, and by approaching them with curiosity and a sense of wonder, you can find joy in the most unexpected places.

So, dear humans, let your inner Muppet shine through. Embrace the head tilting moments that make you giggle and cherish the moments of innocent curiosity. If your partner passes wind, rather than berate them, tilt your head and appear curious. After all, it's those moments that make life all the more charming and endearing even if they do smell horrible.

With a quizzical head tilt and a heart full of curiosity,

Muppet

CHAPTER 14

PERCY THE PUG'S BOTTOM DRAGGING EXTRAVAGANZA

Yo, humans! I'm Percy, the Pug, and I'm here to shed some light on the mysterious and highly satisfying world of bottom dragging. But before we dive into this dark art, let me assure you, it's not as scandalous as it may sound.

You see, we dogs have our own unique way of getting things done, and for me, bottom dragging is a work of art. It's a way to assert my dominance over the grassy terrain or the cosy carpet. And yes, I choose the most inconvenient moments to indulge in this delightful habit.

The level of satisfaction I derive from it is simply unparalleled. The way I can circle and drag my bottom in a perfectly orchestrated routine is a marvel to behold. It's like my own little dance of triumph, a declaration of my presence and individuality.

Now, let's talk about timing. Humans, you may wonder why I often choose the most inconvenient moments to engage in this dark art. Well, it's all part of the fun! When you're wrapped up in an important phone call or engrossed in your favorite

TV show, my bottom dragging serves as a gentle reminder that life is full of surprises.

And now, for the 'Waggy Tailed Wisdom' I'd like to share with you. Bottom dragging, in all its eccentricity, is a lesson in embracing life's quirks and finding humour in unexpected moments. In your world, remember that life isn't always about sticking to a rigid plan.

Sometimes, it's the unexpected detours and moments of silliness that add spice to your journey. Embrace the inconveniences and find joy in the little surprises that come your way. Just as I revel in the satisfaction of my bottom dragging extravaganza, you can find contentment in life's unplanned adventures.

So, dear humans, let your inner Percy shine through. Don't be afraid to step out of your comfort zone, to indulge in a bit of whimsy, and to appreciate the unconventional aspects of life. You might even desire to attempt some of your own bottom-dragging escapades. After all, it's these quirks that make life truly extraordinary.

With a twirl and a drag,

Percy

CHAPTER 15

RALPH THE ROTTWEILER'S STINK-ROLLING ADVENTURES

Hey, hey, hey, humans! I'm Ralph, the Rottweiler, and today, I'm here to uncover the mysteries behind one of our most peculiar habits - rolling in something stinky. You may wonder why we do it, and trust me, it's more than just a dirty deed.

First, let's address the "why" behind this rather aromatic behaviour. You see, it's all about indulging in the moment. When I stumble upon a foul-smelling substance, be it poop or a deceased critter, my instincts kick in, and I can't help but immerse myself in it.

Why, you ask? Well, it's a connection to my primal ancestry. In the wild, the pack had to rely on a common scent to identify one another. Rolling in something stinky was our way of blending in with the group, masking our individual scent, and becoming one with the pack. It's like donning a disguise to become a true member of the tribe.

So, when I roll in that putrid perfume, it's not just about the stink; it's about embracing my ancient heritage and reconnecting with the roots of my canine identity. And yes, I'm aware it's not the most pleasant perfume for you humans, but for us, it's a scent of camaraderie.

Now, for the 'Waggy Tailed Wisdom' I'd like to impart. Rolling in something stinky may seem baffling to you, but it's a lesson in embracing your own history and connecting with your roots. In your world, don't shy away from the aspects of your past that have shaped you.

Find ways to honour your heritage, whether it's through traditions, stories, or simply taking a moment to reflect on where you came from. Just as I revel in the stinky delights of my ancestors, you can find fulfilment in acknowledging and preserving your own history.

So, dear humans, let your inner Ralph shine through. Embrace the unique scent of your own heritage and celebrate the traditions that have shaped you. And remember, it's the quirks and the scents of your past that make you who you are today.

With a hearty roll and a stinky grin,

Ralph

CHAPTER 16

PADDY THE DACHSHUND'S TREAT TEMPTATIONS

Hello, dear humans! I'm Paddy, the Dachshund, and if there's one thing that makes my heart race and my tail wag with unbridled excitement, it's treats. You might say I'm treat-obsessed, and I wouldn't argue with you for a second.

You see, treats are the ultimate motivators in my life. They're the magical keys to my heart, and I'll do just about anything to earn a tasty morsel. From the moment I catch the scent of a treat, I become a determined and sometimes stubborn little fellow.

When my owner holds a treat before me, I'll sit, stay, roll over, or even perform intricate dance moves with undeniable precision. And you can bet that my short legs are surprisingly nimble when there's a treat involved.

But why are treats so irresistible, you ask? Well, it's a matter of pure joy and anticipation. The moment I sink my teeth into that delicious morsel, it's as if a burst of happiness erupts within me. It's a feeling of instant gratification, a reward for my efforts, and I savour every bite.

Now, for the 'Waggy Tailed Wisdom' I'd like to impart. Treat time is more than just a snack; it's a reminder to embrace life's simple pleasures. In your world, find your own "treats" - those moments of pure delight and indulgence.

Whether it's savouring your favourite dessert, enjoying a cosy afternoon with a good book, or relishing a warm cup of tea, treat time is an essential part of life. It's a way to reward yourself for your hard work and dedication and to savour the sweet moments life offers.

So, dear humans, let your inner Paddy shine through. Don't be afraid to indulge in your own "treats" and relish the joy they bring. Treat time is a reminder to celebrate the little joys that make life truly delicious. In fact, why not get 'treat-tastic' and allow yourself some joy now…

With a wagging tail and a treat-filled heart,

Paddy

CHAPTER 17

CRUMPET THE GOLDEN RETRIEVER - THE DINNER TABLE BANDIT

Greetings, my fellow food enthusiasts! I'm Crumpet, a Golden Retriever with an insatiable love for all things edible. If there's a tasty morsel within my reach, you can bet I'll stop at nothing to snag it. I am, without a doubt, the classic dinner table bandit.

Let's start with the picnic raids. Oh, the delight of bounding into a park and discovering a picnic in progress! It's a treasure trove of tantalising aromas and delectable dishes just waiting to be explored. I've honed my picnic raid skills to perfection.

With a swift dash and an irresistible smile, I can charm even the sternest of picnickers into sharing their snacks. I've perfected the art of drooling techniques under the table, and trust me, it's an art form that can't be underestimated. The mere hint of a crumb, a cheese slice, or a hot dog, and I'm on it like a food-loving tornado.

But my food-stealing adventures don't end at picnics. Oh no, I've developed a knack for raiding the dinner table as well. When no one is looking, I employ my stealthy skills and snatch a bite of whatever delectable dish is on offer. It's a talent that requires timing, patience, and, of course, a wagging tail to distract from my cunning endeavours.

And let's not forget the audacity of raiding other dog's bowls if they're silly enough to leave their din-dins unattended. A quick swap of bowls, and I'm enjoying a second helping while they wonder where their meal disappeared to. It's all in good fun, of course!

Now, for the 'Waggy Tailed Wisdom' I'd like to impart. Food stealing, in all its delicious audacity, is a reminder to savour life's indulgent moments. In your world, don't be afraid to treat yourself to a little culinary adventure now and then.

Whether it's trying a new restaurant, indulging in your favourite dessert, or simply savouring a home-cooked meal with loved ones, food brings people together and creates lasting memories. Just as I delight in the aftermath of a successful food heist, you can find joy in savouring the flavours of life.

So, dear humans, let your inner Crumpet shine through. Embrace the culinary delights that surround you and create moments of indulgence that make life all the more flavourful. After all, the joy of food is meant to be shared and celebrated.

With a gleam in my eye and a growling tummy,

Crumpet

CHAPTER 18

HARRY THE HUSKY - THE FETCHING EXTRAORDINAIRE

Aloha, humans! I'm Harry, the Husky, and if there's one thing I excel at, it's fetching. But not just the usual stuff like tennis balls or sticks; oh no, I have a talent for fetching everything and anything from the most peculiar places.

Let's start with some examples. Picture this: a remote control, seemingly lost forever between the sofa cushions. To you, it might be a lost cause, but to me, it's a challenge. With determination in my eyes and a wagging tail, I dive headfirst into the cushions and emerge triumphantly, remote in tow.

Or how about a single sock? Humans, you often wonder where the other sock has gone, but I know precisely where it is - hidden away in the laundry basket. I've perfected the art of sock retrieval, making sure to bring it back with just the right amount of slobber for that extra touch of authenticity.

But my fetching adventures don't stop there. Oh, no. I've been known to fetch newspapers, toys that have mysteriously disappeared under the furniture, and even the occasional dish towel that slipped from the kitchen counter. If it's within my reach, it's fair game for fetching.

Now, for the 'Fun-tastic Waggy Tailed Wisdom' I'd like to impart. My fetching escapades teach us all a valuable lesson - the joy of embracing unexpected surprises. In your world, don't be afraid to explore the hidden treasures that life presents.

Sometimes, the most delightful moments come from the unexpected, whether it's finding a forgotten book on your shelf, stumbling upon a hidden gem in a thrift store, or simply enjoying a spontaneous adventure. Just as I revel in the joy of fetching the unexpected, you can find happiness in the unexpected moments that life has to offer.

So, dear humans, let your inner Harry shine through. Embrace the spontaneity of life, explore the nooks and crannies, and be open to the delightful surprises that await you. After all, it's the unexpected that often brings the most laughter and joy.

With a playful bark and a wagging tail,

Harry

CHAPTER 19

TERRY THE BOXER - THE SLOBBER MAESTRO

Hey there, folks! I'm Terry, the Boxer, and I'm here to school you on the art of drool, slobber, and the incredible joy they bring. You see, I'm a bit of a slobber maestro, and I wear my slobbery badge with pride.

Now, let's talk about drool. It can be caused by many things, like the delicious scent of a juicy steak or the anticipation of a good belly rub. But for me, it's not just a reaction; it's a source of sheer delight. When I feel that slobbery sensation welling up inside, I know I'm about to embark on a slobberific adventure.

Ah, the joy of the slobber release! It's like a symphony of saliva, a dance of droplets that brings a smile to my face. Whether it's a gentle trickle or a full-blown slobber shower, I revel in the sensation, and I'm not afraid to flaunt it.

But here's where the fun gets even slobberier - the legendary "Drool-Off." Picture this: a gathering of fellow drooly dogs, all ready to showcase their slobbering skills. We take turns, one by one, releasing our slobber in glorious splatters. It's a sight to behold, and the winner gets the coveted title of "Slobber King."

Now, for the 'Waggy Tailed Wisdom' I'd like to impart. Slobber, as messy as it may seem, is a reminder to let loose and embrace the messy, unpredictable side of life. In your world, don't be afraid to get a little messy now and then, to let go of inhibitions, and to savour the moments that make you feel truly alive.

Life is not always neat and tidy, and that's perfectly okay. Just as I find joy in the slobbery chaos of a "Drool-Off," you can find happiness in the unscripted moments that make life rich and unforgettable.

So, dear humans, let your inner Terry shine through. Embrace the slobbery surprises that come your way, and remember that sometimes, the messiest moments are the ones that leave you with the biggest smile.

With a slobbery shake and a wagging tail,

Terry

CHAPTER 20

BOB THE BASSET HOUND - SOCK ENTHUSIAST EXTRAORDINAIRE

Top of the sock morning to you, my fellow sock aficionados! I'm Bob, the Basset Hound, and I'm here to share with you the undeniable love and joy that socks can bring into a dog's life. Trust me, there's more to socks than meets the eye.

Let's start with the basics - the wet socks. You humans might cringe at the thought, but for us dogs, a wet sock is like a treasure trove of earthy scents and damp delights. Whether it's from a romp in the rain or a misadventure in a puddle, wet socks are a source of endless fascination.

Now, onto the stinky socks. Oh, the aroma! To you, they might be offensive, but to me, they're like a symphony of scents. A stinky sock tells the tale of your adventures, from long walks in the park to cosy evenings by the fire. I revel in their fragrant history.

And then, there are the holey socks. Humans, you may see them as worn-out and useless, but to me, they're an invitation to play. A holey sock becomes the perfect tug-of-war partner, offering hours of amusement and bonding with my beloved humans.

But wait, there's more! Socks can also bring about the joy of the sock tug. Whether it's a friendly game with a fellow canine companion or a spirited match with my human, the excitement of tugging on a sock is an experience like no other.

Now, for the 'Waggy Tailed Wisdom' I'd like to impart. Socks, in all their wet, stinky, and holey glory, are a reminder to find joy in the simple pleasures of life. In your world, don't overlook the everyday moments that can bring a smile to your face.

Whether it's the smell of fresh laundry, the warmth of a cosy pair of socks, or the shared laughter during a friendly game, simple joys can create lasting memories. Just as I cherish my wet, stinky, and holey socks, you can find happiness in the ordinary moments that make life extraordinary.

So, dear humans, let your inner Bob shine through. Embrace the quirks and simple delights that surround you, and remember that sometimes, it's the everyday joys that bring the most laughter and warmth.

With floppy ears and a wagging tail,

Bob

CHAPTER 21

SHEILA THE SHIH TZU - THE MASTER OF PUPPY MISCHIEF

Hi, hi, hi, dear friends! I'm Sheila, the Shih Tzu, and I have a confession to make - I am a master of puppy mischief, especially when it comes to chewing and destroying everything in sight. But let me assure you, my destructive endeavours are all in the name of canine curiosity!

Let's start with shoes. Ah, the allure of a freshly worn pair of sneakers or a fancy leather shoe! I couldn't resist the temptation to give them a good chew. You see, in the world of a puppy, shoes are like chewy treasures, and I simply had to explore their taste and texture.

And then there are flip flops. Those colourful, rubbery delights practically begged to be chewed. I had to investigate their bouncy properties, and, well, let's just say that flip flops don't bounce back quite the same way after a puppy investigation.

Cushions, oh cushions! They are like fluffy clouds just waiting to be transformed by a puppy's playful paws and sharp little teeth. I saw it as my duty to give those cushions a makeover, adding extra fluff and character in the process.

Now, onto the 'Waggy Tailed Wisdom' I'd like to impart. Puppy mischief, as mischievous as it may seem, is a reminder to embrace your curiosity and explore the world around you. In your world, don't be afraid to follow your instincts, even if it means breaking a few metaphorical cushions along the way.

Curiosity fuels creativity, and sometimes, it takes a playful exploration to discover new perspectives and ideas. Just as I found joy in chewing and destroying, you can find happiness in the journey of exploration and self-discovery.

So, dear humans, let your inner Sheila shine through. Embrace your curiosity, take those little leaps of faith, and remember that sometimes, it's the playful misadventures that lead to the most delightful discoveries.

With a wagging tail and a mischievous grin,

Sheila

CHAPTER 22

MIKE THE MASTIFF – THE WHIZZ OF RANDOM CHEWS

Woooooof, folks! I'm Mike, the Mastiff, and I have a secret hobby that I'm about to reveal - the world of random chews and the mysterious hiding of pig's ears. But fear not, my dear humans; there's a method to my madness.

Let's start with the random chews. You see, I have an insatiable desire to explore the textures of life, and sometimes that leads to, well, unexpected places. Like the corner of a table or the leg of a chair. In my world, every nook and cranny is a potential chew toy, and I am determined to leave no surface unchewed.

Now, onto the pig's ears. Those delectable treats are like hidden treasures waiting to be discovered. I carefully select the perfect hiding spots, whether it's under the bed, nestled in the sofa cushions, or even on the pillow of the bed. It's my way of creating a game of hide and seek, with pig's ears as the prise.

But why, you might ask? It's all about the joy of the hunt and the satisfaction of discovery. Each pig's ear is a delightful surprise waiting to be found, and the thrill of the search is what keeps me entertained.

Now, for the 'Waggy Tailed Wisdom' I'd like to share. Random chews and hidden pig's ears remind us to find joy in the unexpected moments of life. In your world, don't be afraid to embrace the element of surprise. If you discover a pig's ear on your pillow, then embrace it. Yes, it is a surprise, but it shows that the universe can deliver the unexpected when you least expect it!

Sometimes, the most delightful discoveries come from unknown sources and completely by accident, whether it's stumbling upon a hidden gem in an antique shop or finding inspiration in the ordinary. Just as I find happiness in my random chews and hidden treasures, you can find joy in the unpredictable wonders of life.

So, dear humans, let your inner Mike shine through. Embrace the unexpected, explore the world around you with curiosity, and remember that sometimes, it's the spontaneous moments that lead to the greatest adventures.

With a wagging tail and a twinkle in my eye,

Mike

CHAPTER 23

RUBY THE POINTER - THE DIGGER AND HIDER EXTRAORDINAIRE

Hello, everyone! I'm Ruby, the Pointer, and I have a passion for digging and hiding things that I'd love to share with you. You see, there's more to these muddy paws and sandy snouts than meets the eye.

Let's start with mud digging. There's something incredibly satisfying about sinking my paws into soft, cool mud. It's like Mother Nature's playground just waiting for me to explore. And when I dig, oh boy, it's not just about making a mess; it's about unearthing the hidden treasures of the earth.

Now, onto sand digging. The beach is my happy place, and the sandy shores are my canvas. I use my paws to create intricate designs, sculpting the sand into marvellous shapes. And sometimes, I'll bury things, like seashells or even a favorite toy, as a playful surprise for later.

But why, you might wonder? It's all about the thrill of discovery and the joy of the hunt. When I hide a treasure, whether it's a bone, a toy, or even a stick, it becomes a secret waiting to be uncovered. And the excitement of finding it again is a celebration of my canine ingenuity.

Now, for the 'Waggy Tailed Wisdom' I'd like to impart. Digging and hiding things remind us to connect with our primal instincts and embrace the sense of adventure. In your world, don't be afraid to get your hands dirty, metaphorically speaking.

Explore new territories, try your hand at creative endeavours, and don't hesitate to hide a little treasure of your own. Just as I find joy in digging and discovering, you can find happiness in the journey of exploration and the satisfaction of unearthing hidden gems.

So, dear humans, let your inner Ruby shine through. Embrace the spirit of curiosity, venture into the unknown, and remember that sometimes, the most rewarding treasures are those you uncover along the way.

With a wagging tail and a muddy nose,

Ruby

CHAPTER 24

THE MALTESE MARVEL - A LAP DOG'S GUIDE TO AFFECTION

Ta daaaaa, dear friends! I'm the Maltese Marvel, and I'm here to share the secrets of affection from a lap dog's point of view. You see, I was born to cuddle, kiss, and bask in the behind-the-ear delights.

First things first, being on a lap is my natural habitat. You could say I was designed for it. Whether it's the soft lap of my beloved human or a cosy blanket, I find solace in the warmth and companionship of a lap. It's where I truly belong.

Cuddles and kisses? Oh, they are the highlight of my day. The gentle embrace of loving arms and the sweet pecks on my tiny nose fill my heart with joy. For us Maltese lap dogs, affection is more than just a gesture; it's a language of love that knows no bounds.

And let's not forget the behind-the-ear delight. There's something magical about having those velvety ears scratched and caressed. It's pure bliss, and it's one of the ways my humans and I bond on a deeper level. The ear rubs are like our secret handshake.

But what can humans learn from us? The 'Waggy Tailed Wisdom' is this: Affection is a powerful force that brings hearts closer. In your world, don't hold back when it comes to showing love and appreciation.

Embrace the power of a warm hug, a loving kiss, or a kind word. Expressing affection not only strengthens bonds but also spreads warmth and happiness. Just as I thrive in a lap of love, you can nurture your relationships through the simple act of showing you care.

So, dear humans, let your inner Maltese Marvel shine through. Embrace affection with an open heart, and remember that the language of love is universal, transcending species and bringing joy to all.

With a wagging tail and a heart full of love,

The Maltese Marvel

CHAPTER 25

COLIN THE CAVAPOO - THE MASTER OF HILARIOUS SNEEZES

Hello, dear friends! I'm Colin, the Cavapoo, and I'm here to share my secret talent with you - the art of the hilarious sneeze. You see, I've perfected this craft over the years, and it never fails to catch everyone off guard.

First things first, the doggy sneeze is an art form. It requires perfect timing and a bit of flair. I like to build up the suspense, sniffing around as if I'm on a mission, and then, when no one expects it, I let out a big, unexpected ACHOO! It's my way of keeping life exciting.

Now, onto the nose-rubbing. After a good sneeze, my nose often feels a bit ticklish, so I have to rub it on everything I can find. Bristly welcome mats are my personal favorite. There's something oddly satisfying about the sensation, and it's my way of leaving my mark on the world, one bristle at a time.

But why do I do it, you might wonder? It's all about the joy of spontaneity and the element of surprise. Life can sometimes get a bit routine, and my sneezes are a reminder that there's beauty in the unexpected moments.

Now, for the 'Waggy Tailed Wisdom' I'd like to share. Hilarious sneezes and nose-rubbing antics remind us to find humour in the everyday and embrace the joy of spontaneity. In your world, don't be afraid to let loose and be a little unpredictable.

Laugh at life's quirks, enjoy the unexpected surprises, and remember that sometimes, the most memorable moments are the ones that catch you off guard. Just as I revel in my sneezing artistry, you can find happiness in the whimsical moments that life has to offer.

So, dear humans, let your inner Colin shine through. Embrace the art of spontaneity and humour and remember that a good laugh is the best remedy for a routine day.

With a wagging tail and a mischievous grin,

Colin

CHAPTER 26

DELILA THE GREAT DANE - QUEEN OF FURNITURE STEALING

Good day, everyone! I'm Delila, the Great Dane, and I must confess—I have a talent for furniture stealing that knows no bounds. From couches to comfy beds, I believe that if it looks cosy, it's fair game for a dog of my stature.

First things first, I take the term "lap dog" to a whole new level. When I see a vacant spot on the couch, I don't hesitate to claim it as my throne. Sometimes, I even attempt to sit on my beloved human if they're occupying my chosen spot. After all, it's all about maximising comfort, right?

Now, when it comes to comfy beds, I believe in the principle of "more is more." I stretch out to my full majestic length, often spilling over the edges. But who can blame me? It's the perfect way to ensure a good night's sleep. Besides, my humans can always find a corner to curl up in.

But why do I do it, you might wonder? It's all about the joy of indulgence and the comfort of home. My furniture-stealing escapades are a testament to the simple pleasures of life. Sometimes, all you need is a soft spot to call your own.

Now, for the 'Waggy Tailed Wisdom' I'd like to share. Furniture stealing reminds us to appreciate the little indulgences and comforts of home. In your world, don't be afraid to create your own cosy oasis.

Whether it's a favourite chair, a warm blanket, or a well-loved spot on the couch, take time to savour the simple joys of relaxation. Just as I revel in my furniture-stealing adventures, you can find happiness in the sanctuary of your own home and the comfort it provides.

So, dear humans, let your inner Delila shine through. Embrace the art of relaxation and the joy of claiming your own cosy spot, and remember that sometimes, the most treasured moments are the ones spent in comfort.

With a wagging tail and a regal demeanour,

Delila

CHAPTER 27

GLORIA THE GREYHOUND - IN PURSUIT OF THE INVISIBLE

Greetings, dear friends! I'm Gloria, the Greyhound, and I have a secret passion that some might call peculiar—I am an avid connoisseur of the invisible. You see, there is a world of delights that capture my attention, and they exist solely in the realm of the unseen.

First things first, let's talk about the invisible treats. You may see me standing there, seemingly licking the air for no apparent reason, but in my world, I am savouring the taste of the ethereal. These invisible morsels are like the finest delicacies, and my palate knows no bounds when it comes to savouring them.

Now, why do I do it, you might wonder? It's all about the joy of imagination and the thrill of the unknown. The invisible treats that I taste are the stuff of dreams, and they transport me to a world where anything is possible. In that moment, I am not just a Greyhound; I am an explorer of the limitless.

But what can humans learn from my peculiar passion? The 'Waggy Tailed Wisdom' is this: Embrace the wonder of the unknown. In your world, don't be afraid to imagine and dream beyond the visible. Sometimes, the most extraordinary experiences are the ones that exist only in the realm of your imagination.

Discover the magic in everyday moments, and let your creativity roam free. Just as I indulge in the pursuit of the invisible, you can find joy in the limitless possibilities that your imagination offers.

So, dear humans, let your inner Gloria shine through. Embrace the art of imagination and remember that the unseen can be as delightful as the visible. After all, the world is full of wonders, both real and imaginary.

With a wagging tail and a twinkle in my eye,

Gloria

CHAPTER 28

PERRY THE PEKINGESE - THE ART OF GIFT-GIVING

Hello, dear friends! I'm Perry, the Pekingese, and I must say, I have a talent for gift-giving that often leaves my humans both bewildered and amused. You see, I have an impeccable sense of timing when it comes to delivering surprises.

First things first, let's talk about the "gifts" I bring. Now, most dogs might choose to fetch a toy or a sock, but I, Perry, have a flair for the dramatic. Picture this: a quiet evening, my humans entertaining guests, and there I am, strutting proudly into the room with a pair of used underwear dangling from my mouth. Oh, the gasps and laughter that ensue!

Now, you might wonder why I do it. It's all about the joy of sharing and the art of making people smile. My "gifts" are not just random items; they're tokens of my love and devotion. I believe in spreading laughter and brightening the day, even if it means a few blushes.

But what can humans learn from my unique gift-giving skills? The 'Waggy Tailed Wisdom' is this: Embrace the unexpected with a smile. In your world, don't be afraid to inject a little humour into the everyday.

Life is full of surprises, and sometimes, the quirkiest moments are the ones that create lasting memories. What do you expect if you leave your dirty undies in grabbing distance or on the floor? So, my dear humans, when life hands you used underwear, find the humour in the situation, and let it be a reminder that laughter is the best gift of all.

With a wagging tail and a penchant for surprises,

Perry

CHAPTER 29

SPROUT THE YORKSHIRE TERRIER - CHASING THE ELUSIVE REFLECTION

Woooooof, everyone! I'm Sprout, the Yorkshire Terrier, and I have a story to share about the curious world of reflections. You see, there's something about that elusive "other dog" in the mirror that keeps me endlessly entertained.

First things first, let's talk about the mirror. When I glance into it, I'm convinced that there's a furry, mischievous Yorkshire Terrier on the other side, just waiting to play. I pounce, I bark, I spin in circles—all in an attempt to catch that tricky reflection.

But why do I do it, you might wonder? It's all about the joy of discovery and the thrill of the chase. I can't help myself; the reflection calls to me like a playful friend. It's as if there's a secret world on the other side of the glass, and I must explore it.

Now, let's add a little tale from the doggy history books. You may have heard of a fellow named Narcissus, a human who fell in love with his own reflection. Well, I like to think that I'm giving him a lesson in canine charm. I chase my reflection not out of vanity, but out of sheer delight.

So, what's the 'Waggy Tailed Wisdom' here? Embrace the simple joys of curiosity and play. In your world, don't be afraid to chase your own reflections, whether they're in a mirror or in the opportunities life presents.

Just as I find endless amusement in my mirror adventures, you can find fulfilment in the pursuit of your passions and the discovery of new horizons. Life is full of playful moments waiting to be explored, so go ahead and chase your own reflections with enthusiasm.

With a wagging tail and a curious spirit,

Sprout

CHAPTER 30

BETTY THE BLOODHOUND - WIND IN MY FUR AND A BIG DOGGY SMILE

Good day to you all! I'm Betty, the loose-lipped Bloodhound, and today I want to share with you one of life's greatest pleasures: sticking my head out of the car window. It's an adventure like no other, and I wouldn't trade it for all the bones in the world.

Now, picture this: the car door opens, and I hop in with a heart full of excitement. I know what's coming next. As the engine roars to life, I can hardly contain myself. My nose twitches, my ears flap in the wind, and my lips flap like flags in a parade. Oh, the sheer delight!

As we hit the open road, I stick my head out the window, and suddenly, I'm not just a Bloodhound; I'm a free spirit on an epic journey. The wind ruffles my fur, and I can smell a world of scents, from freshly mowed grass to sizzling barbecue. It's like a buffet for my nose!

But why do I do it, you might ask? It's all about the exhilaration of the moment. In those precious seconds, I'm living life to the fullest, and the world rushes by in a blur of sights and smells. It's a reminder that there's so much beauty and adventure out there, just waiting to be discovered.

Now, let's talk about the 'Waggy Tailed Wisdom' I'd like to share. Embrace the simple pleasures that life offers. In your world, take a moment to stick your head out of your own "window" metaphorically. Feel the wind in your hair (or in your imagination), and let go of worries, if only for a while.

Life is a grand journey, and it's important to savour the moments that make you feel truly alive. So, my dear humans, roll down the windows of your own life, let the wind in, and wear a big, doggy smile. Adventure awaits just around the corner.

With a wagging tail and a zest for life,

Betty

CHAPTER 31

BRENDA THE BOLOGNESE - THE ART OF TOY THEFT

Ciao, Ciao, dear humans! I'm Brenda, the Bolognese, and I have a tale to tell you about the mischievous world of toy theft. You see, in my home, I live with Terence, the Terrier, and together, we've turned toy theft into an art form.

First things first, let me introduce you to Terence. He's a spunky little fellow with a penchant for toys. Now, I must admit, I can't resist a good game of tug-of-war, and Terence's toys just happen to be the perfect match for my size. So, naturally, I borrow them from time to time.

But why do I do it, you might wonder? It's all about play and camaraderie. Terence and I engage in epic battles over our shared toys, and it's all in good fun. We chase, we tussle, and we bond over the joy of playtime.

Now, you might be curious about the 'Waggy Tailed Wisdom' I have to offer. It's this: Embrace the spirit of play and sharing. In your world, don't be afraid to share the toys of life, whether they're physical possessions or moments of joy.

Just as Terence and I find laughter and connection through our playful thievery, you can find fulfilment in sharing your joys with others. Life is more enjoyable when you can engage in a little playful competition while building bonds that last a lifetime.

So, my dear humans, let your inner Brenda shine, and remember that sharing is caring, especially when it comes to the toys of life.

With a wagging tail and a playful spirit,

Brenda

CHAPTER 32

DARRYL THE DREVER - THRIVING IN A PACK

Hey there, lovely humans! I'm Darryl, the Drever, and I've got a tail-wagging story to share about my life with my incredible pack of rescue dogs. Each member of our pack has a unique tale to tell, and together, we've discovered the true meaning of family.

First, let me introduce you to my fellow pack members:

Luna, the Lurcher from Ireland: She's our graceful and swift leader, with a heart as big as her leaps.

Rex, the Rottweiler from Germany: Despite his imposing size, Rex is a gentle giant who's always ready to protect his pack.

Mila, the Maltese from Greece: A petite pup with a big personality, Mila adds a touch of elegance to our pack.

Leo, the Labrador from the USA: Leo's boundless energy and friendly nature keep us all active and smiling.

Kiko, the Keeshond from the Netherlands: Kiko's fluffy coat and unwavering loyalty make him the heart of our pack.

Now, you might be wondering how this diverse group of dogs from different countries came together to form a pack. It's simple, really—rescue brought us together. Each of us had our own struggles and hardships until we found our forever home with our loving human.

Being part of a pack is a bit like being part of a big, bustling family. We play together, eat together, and even curl up for naps together. But it's more than just sharing a space; it's about sharing our hearts. We've learned the true meaning of trust, loyalty, and unconditional love.

Our pack mentality has taught us many valuable lessons, and we'd like to share them with you through some "Waggy Tailed Wisdom":

Embrace Diversity: In our pack, we come from different backgrounds and have unique personalities, but that's what makes us strong. Embrace the diversity around you; it enriches your life.

Family Is What You Make It: Family isn't just about blood; it's about the bonds you create. Whether it's friends, pets, or even colleagues, the connections you nurture become your chosen family.

Support and Loyalty: We've got each other's backs through thick and thin. Loyalty and support create a strong foundation for any pack.

Live in the Moment: Dogs have a knack for living in the present, enjoying every moment. Try to embrace the present, and you'll find more joy in your everyday life.

Rescue and Adopt: Our pack was formed through rescue and adoption, and we believe every pet deserves a loving home. Consider adopting a pet in need and change a life forever.

So, my dear humans, take a page from our pack's book and cherish the bonds you create with others. Find strength in your diversity, support each other through thick and thin, and remember that family is what you make it.

With a wagging tail and a heart full of love,

Darryl and the Pack

CHAPTER 33

RUFUS'S WISDOM - THE ART OF THE "TUM TUM"

Sniff, sniff and tail wagging, dear humans! I'm Rufus, Ruby's pup, the multi-Cocka-poo Shih Tzu, and I'm here to share with you the profound wisdom that lies within the simple act of the "tum tum," also known as the belly rub.

You see, the "tum tum" is not just any ordinary belly rub; it's a sacred exchange of love and trust between humans and dogs. Allow me to shed some light on how to lure your owner into this divine experience:

Step 1: The Pose - It all starts with the pose. Find a cosy spot, lie on your back, and expose your soft, fluffy belly to the world. This is the universal sign that says, "I'm ready for some belly rub magic!"

Step 2: The Pleading Eyes - Lock your eyes onto your human's soul and let them see your longing for the ultimate "tum tum." Trust me; this step is essential for success.

Step 3: The Soft Whine - A gentle, soft whine can work wonders. It's like music to their ears, and it'll melt their heart faster than you can say "tummy."

Step 4: The Strategic Wiggle - Gently wiggle your paws and tail. It's a subtle invitation that says, "Come on, I can't wait any longer!"

Now, once you've successfully lured your human into the "tum tum" experience, both parties can truly enjoy it. Humans, here's your role:

1. The Gentle Touch: Approach your dog with care and tenderness. Use your fingers to caress their belly gently. Avoid tickling; remember, it's about relaxation, not laughter.

2. The Connection: Look into your dog's eyes and create a deep connection. This is a moment of bonding and trust-building.

3. The Sweet Talk: Speak softly and lovingly to your furry friend. Let them know how much you adore them.

Now, let's get to the heart of the matter—the profound wisdom of the "tum tum." You see, in this simple act of trust and affection, we discover the true meaning of life. It's a reminder that life is meant to be lived in moments of pure joy, connection, and vulnerability.

The "tum tum" teaches us that happiness can be found in the simple pleasures, in the warmth of a loving touch, and in the shared connection between humans and dogs.

So, my dear humans, embrace the "tum tum" with your furry companions. Cherish these moments of connection and vulnerability, for in them, you'll find the profound wisdom that life is meant to be lived in love and joy.

With a wagging tail and an open heart,

Rufus

CHAPTER 34

JEFF'S DREAMLAND ADVENTURES

THE ART OF RUNNING IN THEIR SLEEP

Hey there, folks! I'm Jeff, the Jack Russell, and I'm here to take you on a journey into the whimsical world of running in our sleep. You've probably seen us do it—legs paddling furiously, funny barks escaping our dreamy lips, and the occasional twitch or jerk that makes you wonder what we're chasing in our dreams.

First things first, let's address the basics. When we embark on these nocturnal adventures, we're not just snoozing; we're diving headfirst into a dreamland of excitement. Ever notice how our paws move as if we're sprinting after the most tantalising squirrel or the fleetest of tennis balls? That's because, in our dreams, we're the canine champions of chase!

Now, let's dive into the enchanting world of running in our sleep, complete with a few insights and waggy-tailed wisdom:

1. Dreamy Escapades: Imagine, for a moment, that you're chasing butterflies through a sun-dappled meadow or sprinting across a sandy beach with the wind in your fur. That's precisely what we

experience during these sleep adventures. It's a reminder that even in our slumber, we're living life to the fullest.

2. Unbridled Joy: Have you ever noticed the ecstatic expressions on our faces as we race through dreamscapes? That's pure joy in its unfiltered form. Our dreams serve as a joyful escape, a reminder to savour life's moments and find excitement in the ordinary.

3. Mystery and Imagination: As we run, bark, and twitch in our sleep, it's a testament to the power of our imagination. We're creators of our own dreamworlds, where anything is possible. It's a gentle nudge for you humans to embrace your own creativity and explore the unknown.

4. Recharge and Rejuvenate: Our dreams aren't just entertaining; they're also essential for our well-being. Running in our sleep helps us recharge, process experiences, and prepare for new adventures when we wake up. It's a reminder to prioritise rest and rejuvenation in your own lives.

Waggy-Tailed Wisdom: So, what can you humans learn from our dreamy escapades? Embrace the childlike wonder within you. Allow yourself to dream, to chase after your own aspirations with unbridled enthusiasm. Find joy in the simple pleasures and remember that life is a grand adventure waiting to be explored—both in your waking hours and in your dreams.

With a wagging tail and a dreamy spirit,

Jeff

CHAPTER 35

JASPER'S DOORWAY DILEMMAS - THE MYSTERY OF AUTOMATIC DOORS

Konnichiha, everyone! I'm Jasper, the Japanese Spitz, and I'm here to regale you with my encounters with those perplexing contraptions known as automatic sliding doors. They're like magic portals that open and close with a mind of their own. Join me on this comical journey into the land of confusion!

Picture this: I strut up to the store entrance with an air of canine confidence, ready to embark on a shopping adventure with my human. As we approach, the door remains resolutely shut. I tilt my head, an expression of profound curiosity, as if to say, "Why isn't the magical door opening for me?"

Now, here's where the fun begins. I try to outsmart the door, taking a step forward, then a step back, and then another step forward. It's a delightful dance of confusion, as I contemplate the mysteries of this technological wonder. Is it sentient? Is it teasing me? The possibilities are endless!

But wait, there's more. Sometimes, in my earnest quest to conquer the automatic door, I've been known to accidentally activate it with a paw or a nose bop. The door springs to life, and I react with a delightful blend of surprise and triumph, as if I've just solved a complex puzzle.

Now, for the pièce de résistance—the Waggy-Tailed Wisdom:

Waggy-Tailed Wisdom: You see, dear humans, my encounters with automatic doors are a reminder that life is full of little mysteries and surprises. Embrace the unknown with the same sense of wonder and curiosity that I do when facing these technological marvels.

When faced with a puzzling situation, don't be afraid to tilt your head, ask questions, and explore the unknown with a wagging tail and a heart full of curiosity. Just like me, you might stumble upon unexpected joys and solutions in the process.

So, next time you encounter an automatic door, remember Jasper's antics and let the confusion become an opportunity for laughter and exploration. After all, life's most delightful moments often come when we least expect them.

With a tilted head and a sense of wonder,

Jasper

CHAPTER 36

CANDICE'S CURIOUS CHRONICLES - THE ART OF CROTCH SNIFFING

Sniffy, sniff, sniff, dear humans! I'm Candice, the elegant and ever-curious Chow Chow, here to share with you the intriguing world of crotch sniffing. You see, we dogs have a unique way of gathering information, and it often involves some amusing and occasionally awkward encounters.

Picture me, with my majestic lion-like mane, strolling through the park with my human companion. As we pass by other dogs and their humans, my curiosity awakens. What stories do their scents tell? What secrets are hidden in their crotch areas? It's a world of olfactory exploration!

Now, let's talk about the amusing moments. Sometimes, in my enthusiasm to gather information, I'll approach another dog with a determined sniff. But instead of finding their crotch, I might accidentally land my nose in a rather peculiar place. Oh, the surprised expressions that follow! We all share a good-natured chuckle, as if we're participating in a canine comedy routine.

But there are also the awkward moments. On occasion, I'll encounter a human who is less than thrilled about my investigative prowess. They'll tug on my leash and politely ask me to redirect my curiosity. It's in those moments that I gracefully retreat, wagging my tail as if to say, "No harm done, just a little misunderstanding."

Now, for the Waggy-Tailed Wisdom:

Waggy-Tailed Wisdom: Crotch sniffing may seem peculiar to you humans, but for us dogs, it's a way to connect, understand, and communicate. In our world, scent is a language, and each sniff tells a story. So, when you encounter a dog like me indulging in a bit of crotch exploration, remember that we're simply trying to learn about the world and those who share it with us.

In your own lives, embrace curiosity, and don't shy away from the unfamiliar. Just as we dogs use our keen senses to gather information and connect, you can use your natural curiosity to better understand the people and the world around you. Approach new experiences with an open heart and a wagging spirit, and you might just discover some delightful surprises along the way.

With a nose for knowledge and a heart full of curiosity,

Candice

CHAPTER 37

ALF'S LICK-TASTIC ADVENTURES - SELF-GROOMING SHENANIGANS

Lickity lick, dear humans! I'm Alf, the intrepid West Highland Terrier, here to share with you the fascinating realm of self-licking. We dogs take grooming seriously, and sometimes, we go to great lengths to ensure every nook and cranny is spick and span. Allow me to regale you with tales of my lick-tastic adventures.

First, let's talk about contortion. You humans might marvel at our ability to reach seemingly impossible areas with our tongues. There's no yoga pose too extreme, no acrobatic feat too challenging for us when it comes to self-grooming. Whether it's giving our toes a thorough cleaning or reaching that mysterious spot behind the ear, we're the undisputed masters of flexibility.

Now, about that "we do it because we can" attitude. You see, self-licking is more than just hygiene for us; it's a declaration of independence. We take pride in our ability to tend to our own needs. When we're licking away, it's as if we're saying, "I've got this, human!" We relish the freedom to take charge of our grooming routine.

But there's a flip side to the story. Excessive licking, especially in one area, can sometimes be a sign that something isn't quite right. It could be discomfort, irritation, or even a pesky itch that demands attention. In those cases, it's important for our loving human companions to step in and investigate. A gentle check-up or a visit to the vet might be in order.

Waggy-Tailed Wisdom: While we dogs take pride in our self-licking skills, it's essential for our human friends to keep a watchful eye. Sometimes, our grooming behaviour can be a signal that we need a little extra TLC. Just as you ensure our physical well-being, remember to take time for self-care in your own lives.

Embrace your independence and self-care routines, but also be attuned to your needs and listen to your body. Just as we rely on you to look out for us, take the time to look out for yourselves and those you care about. After all, a little self-love goes a long way in leading a happy and healthy life.

With a tongue for tidiness and a heart for adventure,

Alf

CHAPTER 38

TREAT AND GREET - A WEIMARANER'S PERSPECTIVE

Treat and greetings, dear humans! I'm Wilf, your friendly neighbourhood Weimaraner, and today I'd like to take you on a delightful journey into the world of treats and bones, as seen through my keen canine eyes.

First and foremost, let's talk about bones. Ah, bones—the treasure troves of flavours and textures! You see, bones are more than just tasty morsels for us dogs; they're like a culinary adventure. They satisfy our primal instincts and provide hours of joyful chewing. Not to mention, they're excellent for our dental health, keeping those pearly whites in tip-top shape.

But here's the twist. As much as I adore sinking my teeth into a juicy bone, there's something deep within me that urges me to hide it away. It's an age-old instinct, a remnant of my wild ancestors. In the wild, my forebears had to be resourceful. They'd bury their food to keep it safe from scavengers or to enjoy later when the hunt wasn't as successful.

Now, I'm not exactly battling predators in the living room, but that instinct remains ingrained in me. So,

I'll take that delicious bone you gave me, and off I go on a treasure hunt around the house. I'll dig a little hole in the garden, tuck it behind the sofa, or find the perfect nook in the closet. It's all part of the thrill!

But why do I do it? Well, there's a certain satisfaction in knowing I've got a hidden stash of bones. It's like my own secret treasure trove, and who doesn't love a good secret? Plus, it taps into my natural curiosity and problem-solving skills. Can I find the perfect hiding spot? Can I keep it safe from potential "thieves" (aka other dogs or sneaky siblings)? It's a mental and sensory challenge that keeps me engaged.

Now, let's dive into the 'Waggy Tailed Wisdom' of treat and greet. While you humans might find it amusing (or occasionally perplexing) to discover bones hidden in the strangest places, there's a lesson here. It's a reminder that our furry friends, like me, have instincts and behaviours that harken back to a time when survival was a daily challenge.

So, the next time you stumble upon a hidden bone or a surprise treat tucked away in a corner, take a moment to appreciate the cleverness and resourcefulness of your four-legged companion. It's a small window into our wild heritage, a testament to our adaptability, and a touch of playful mystery in your day.

With a bone between my paws and a wag of my tail,

Wilf

CHAPTER 39

THE PLAYFUL "DOGGY CONGA" - A BULL TERRIER'S PERSPECTIVE

Da, da, da, da, da, daaaa, dear humans! I'm Brian, your friendly Bull Terrier, and today I want to delve into a rather, shall we say, playful topic—the "Doggy Conga," also known as the art of humping, as seen through my enthusiastic canine eyes.

Now, before you chuckle or blush, let me clarify something—this isn't just a boys' club! Yes, male dogs are often associated with humping behaviours, but let me tell you, us ladies are known to join the "conga" too! It's a universal doggy expression of excitement and playfulness.

So, what's the deal with this seemingly odd behaviour? Well, my fellow canines, humping is not solely about romance; it's about communication, social interaction, and sometimes just good old-fashioned fun. When I see a soft, squishy object like my bed or even your leg, an irresistible urge sometimes takes over. It's like an irresistible impulse that says, "I need to engage with this thing, and I need to do it now!"

The truth is humping serves a variety of purposes in our world. It's how we express our excitement, release pent-up energy, and even engage in social play. Think of it as our version of dancing—a bit uncoordinated, perhaps, but always full of enthusiasm!

But Brian, you may ask, why do you feel the need to involve my leg or your bed in this dance of joy? Well, my dear humans, it's because we're having so much fun, and we want to share that joy with the world, or at least with the nearest available object. It's our way of saying, "This moment is so exhilarating, I can't contain myself!"

Now, let's talk about the 'Waggy Tailed Wisdom' we can glean from the "Doggy Conga." As humans, you often strive to find joy in the little things, right? Well, that's precisely what we're doing when we engage in this spirited behaviour. We remind you that there's pleasure to be found in spontaneity and unbridled enthusiasm.

So, the next time you catch us doing the "Doggy Conga," don't be embarrassed or shocked. Instead, remember the simple pleasure of letting loose and embracing the joy of the moment, just like we do. Life is a dance, my friends, and sometimes, it's a playful one filled with exuberance, hide the sausage and a bit of silliness.

With a happy wiggle of my tail,

Brian

CHAPTER 40

BATHROOM BUDDIES: A VIZSLA'S PERSPECTIVE

Well, hello there, dear humans! I'm Verity, your ever-faithful Vizsla companion, and today I'd like to shed some light on a peculiar habit that I believe deserves some attention: our fascination with your bathroom rituals.

You see, it all starts with an unspoken promise, a sacred bond between us and our beloved humans. When you first brought me into your home, we entered into an unspoken agreement: I would be your loyal companion through thick and thin, and in return, you would share every aspect of your life with me, no matter how private.

So, when you make your way to the bathroom, I see it as an invitation, a chance to uphold our end of the bargain. As you close the door behind you, I can't help but wonder, "What mysteries lie behind that closed portal? What adventures await on the other side?"

And so, I follow you faithfully, my toenails clicking on the tiled floor, my tail wagging with excitement. I take my post just outside the bathroom door, ready to offer moral support and unwavering companionship.

Now, you might be wondering why I stare at you with such intensity during this private moment. It's not that I'm judging or critiquing your bathroom habits; quite the opposite, actually. My gaze is filled with admiration and devotion. I'm in awe of your abilities, your multitasking prowess as you juggle various bathroom-related activities.

As you go about your business, you might find my eyes fixed on you, unwavering. It's not a judgmental stare; it's a look of pure adoration. You are my human, and even in these private moments, I'm here to remind you that you're never alone. Your loyal Vizsla is by your side, ready to face whatever challenges the day may bring.

Now, for the "Waggy Tailed Wisdom" that I'd like to share with you humans: Embrace the moments of togetherness, even in the most unexpected places. Life is filled with shared experiences, and it's in these everyday moments that our bonds grow stronger. Whether it's a bathroom rendezvous or a simple walk in the park, cherish the time you spend with your furry companions. We're here to offer love, support, and a reminder that you're never truly alone in this journey of life.

With love and a wagging tail,

Verity

CHAPTER 41

TOILET TIDBITS: A SHAPENDOS'S PERSPECTIVE

Slurpy di slurp, dear humans! I'm Sally, the ever-curious Shapendos, and today I'm here to shed some light on the mysterious allure of toilet bowls and your cups over our regular water bowls.

You see, it's not that we don't appreciate the fresh water you provide us in our designated bowls. It's just that sometimes, the toilet bowl or your cup holds a certain irresistible charm that we can't quite resist. Allow me to explain.

1. The Toilet Bowl Temptation: Ah, the toilet bowl, a porcelain oasis that often holds cool, refreshing water. It's like a secret well of hydration hidden behind a door. When we sneak a sip from the toilet, it's not a rejection of the water you provide; it's more of a "just in case" scenario. What if the water in the bowl is even fresher and cooler than the water in our bowls? We can't resist the temptation to find out.

2. The Cup of Curiosity: Now, your cups, my dear humans, are another story. You carry them around, and they often contain intriguing liquids that pique our curiosity. The scent of your coffee, tea, or even plain water can be quite enticing. It's not that we prefer your cups over our own bowls; it's more about exploring new tastes and smells. Plus, there's something oddly satisfying about drinking from a cup that you've just sipped from. It's like sharing a moment with you, even if you're not in the room.

As for the "Waggy Tailed Wisdom" that I'd like to impart to you humans: Sometimes, our quirks and preferences are simply part of our endearing personalities. While it's essential to ensure our water bowls are clean and fresh, don't take it personally if we occasionally venture into the bathroom or cosy up to your cup. It's a reminder that we're curious creatures, always exploring and seeking new experiences. Embrace these moments, laugh at our antics, and remember that our love for you is as unwavering as our quest for toilet bowl treasures or sips from your cup.

With a wag and a grin,

Sally

CHAPTER 42

MUDDY MARVELS: A MUDI'S PERSPECTIVE

SPLOSH, my fellow mud enthusiasts! I'm Mildred, the Mudi, and today I want to share with you the sheer ecstasy of mud, mud puddles, and the art of coating oneself in nature's finest paste.

1. Mud, Glorious Mud: Oh, the simple joy of mud! To us, mud isn't just a mixture of dirt and water; it's pure happiness. The squelching sound beneath our paws, the cool, earthy sensation on our fur – it's a sensory delight like no other. Mud represents freedom, adventure, and an invitation to embrace the wild side within us.

2. Splish-Splash Splosh: You know what's even more exhilarating than mud? Mud puddles, of course! A fresh mud puddle is a treasure waiting to be explored. We leap in with abandon, sending muddy droplets flying in all directions. The sheer freedom of splashing and sploshing in a puddle is liberating. It's a reminder that life is meant to be lived fully, without hesitation.

3. The Art of Coating: Now, here's where the real magic happens. Coating ourselves in mud isn't just about getting dirty; it's about becoming one with nature. As we roll and wriggle in the mud, it's as if we're painting ourselves with the colours of the earth. Mud becomes our amor, our shield against the mundane. And when we're done, oh, the satisfaction of shaking off the excess, sending mud droplets flying like confetti in a jubilant parade!

Now, for the "Waggy Tailed Wisdom" that I'd like to share with you humans: Don't shy away from life's mud puddles. Embrace the messy, exhilarating moments. Whether it's dancing in the rain, hiking through the wilderness, or simply taking a detour to explore the unknown, relish the opportunities to get a little muddy. It's a reminder that life's most joyful experiences often lie beyond our comfort zones, waiting for us to dive in headfirst.

So, my dear humans, join me in celebrating the muddy marvels of life. Splash in puddles, venture off the beaten path, and don't be afraid to get a little dirty along the way. After all, in the world of mud, the messier, the merrier!

With muddy paws and a heart full of adventure,

Mildred

CHAPTER 43

AVOIDING THE BATH AND EMBRACING THE POST-BATH ZOOMIES

Splish, splosh, splash, my fellow humans! I'm Patricia, the proud Pincer, here to share my perspective on a delightful canine quirk—avoiding baths and the ensuing post-bath zoomies. You see, there's a method to our madness, and it's all part of our furry charm.

First, let's talk about baths. Now, I'm not sure what it is about that tub filled with water, but it sends shivers down my spine. Yes, I'll gleefully wade into a muddy puddle or take a refreshing dip in the river, but a bath? Oh no, it's a different story.

It's as if the bathroom transforms into an impenetrable fortress, and the tub becomes the dreaded watery abyss. I'll employ all my ninja-like skills—hiding under the bed, squeezing into tight corners, and even employing my best puppy-dog eyes to avoid that soapy fate.

But here's the twist: once the bath is over and I'm all clean and fluffy, that's when the magic happens—cue the post-bath zoomies! I race through the house with unbridled enthusiasm, my wet fur flinging droplets in all directions. It's as if the sheer joy of being clean and fresh can't be contained.

So, why the dramatic avoidance and subsequent celebration? Well, it's all about living life to the fullest. We dogs embrace every moment, and sometimes that means savouring the exhilaration of avoiding something we're not particularly fond of (like baths) and then revelling in the newfound freedom of cleanliness.

Now, for the "Waggy Tailed Wisdom" I'd like to impart. Life is full of experiences, both the ones we eagerly embrace and those we might initially resist. Like me, you humans can take a page from our playbook—face the challenges head-on, and when they're behind you, celebrate with all your might.

And remember, the post-challenge celebrations, the joyous moments that follow, can be just as memorable and meaningful as the experiences themselves. So, my dear humans, don't shy away from life's "baths." Embrace them, zoom through the challenges, and bask in the exhilarating moments that follow.

With a zoom and a zing,

Patricia

CHAPTER 44

THE SHAKE - A DOG'S RESET BUTTON

Greetings, my human friends! I'm Larry, the long-haired Pyrenean Shepherd, here to shed some light on a common but fascinating canine behaviour—the shake. You see, we dogs have a secret reset button, and it's located right behind our floppy ears.

First, let's talk about the shake. You might have noticed it when we emerge from a refreshing swim or simply when we've been lounging around for a while. We start with a twitch of the ears, a subtle wiggle, and then the whole-body shake commences. It's like hitting the reset button on a computer, but much more entertaining.

You see, the shake serves several purposes. When we're wet, it helps us get rid of excess water, and it's a bit like a built-in towel to dry ourselves off. But it's not just about getting dry. The shake is also a way for us to reset our senses, shake off any tension, and prepare for what's next.

Now, here's the fun part—the "shaking at people or places." It's not always intentional, you know. Sometimes, we're just so enthusiastic about life that we can't help but share our energy with those around us. So, if you ever find yourself on the receiving end of a spontaneous doggy shake, consider it a compliment. We're simply sharing our zest for life with you.

As for "shaking inconveniently when wet," well, that's just us being true to our nature. We live in the moment, and if a puddle or river beckons, we'll happily dive right in, consequences be darned. After all, what's a little wet fur compared to the sheer joy of a good splash?

Now, for the "Waggy Tailed Wisdom" I'd like to share. Humans, sometimes life can be a bit like a rainstorm—unexpected and messy. But remember, you have your own version of the shake. It might not involve wiggling and water droplets, but it's your way of resetting and embracing what comes next.

So, when things get a bit soggy or chaotic, don't forget to shake it off, just like we do. Let go of the tension, reset your mindset, and dive into the puddles of life with enthusiasm. After all, a little shake can go a long way in brightening your day.

With a shake and a smile,

Larry

CHAPTER 45

LOIS, THE LHASA APSO'S LICKING ADVENTURES

Hello, everyone! I'm Lois, the Lhasa Apso, and I have a delightful tale to share with you about a peculiar but endearing habit—licking behind my owner's ears, bald head licking, and face licking. It's my way of showing love and affection, though it doesn't always go as planned.

Let's start with the ear-licking business. You see, when I get the urge to express my affection, I go for the soft spots behind my owner's ears. It's like a hidden treasure trove of cuddles and snuggles, and I simply can't resist. However, there have been times when my timing was a bit off. Picture this: my owner getting ready for an important meeting, dressed in their finest attire, and there I am, enthusiastically showering them with ear licks. The result? A rather dishevelled, damp human who might be a tad late for their appointment.

Now, onto bald head licking. It's not something I planned on, but sometimes, bald heads are just too tempting to resist. I'm talking about that shiny, smooth surface that practically screams "pet me!" My owner, in all their wisdom, might have chosen to embrace baldness, but I saw it as an invitation to provide an impromptu spa experience. However, my intentions aren't always appreciated, especially when they're trying to have a serious conversation with someone or attend a formal event.

Face licking, on the other hand, is my way of saying, "You're the best thing that ever happened to me!" I can't help but shower my owner's face with affectionate licks, whether they're just waking up or coming home after a long day. But, let's be honest, sometimes my timing is impeccable—like when my owner is in the middle of telling an important story to friends or about to enjoy a romantic dinner.

Now, for the "Waggy Tailed Wisdom" I'd like to offer. Humans, life is full of moments that might not go as planned. Just like my well-intentioned but mistimed licks, sometimes things don't align perfectly. But here's the beauty of it: those imperfect moments often become cherished memories.

So, when life throws you a curveball or a slobbery kiss when you least expect it, embrace it with a smile. After all, it's those unexpected, imperfect moments that add a touch of magic to our lives.

With love and licks,

Lois

CHAPTER 46

FETCHING FUN WITH CYRIL THE IRISH WOLFHOUND

Good day, dear people! I'm Cyril, the proud Irish Wolfhound, and today, I'm going to let you in on a little secret—how I've managed to train my human to play fetch in the most unconventional, delightful way.

You see, fetching is in my blood. It's not just a game; it's a way of life. I've got these long, lanky legs built for chasing, and oh, how I love to chase! So, one day, I decided it was high time to teach my human how to fetch properly.

Step 1: The Launch

I started by choosing the perfect fetching spot—a wide, open field where I could send that ball sailing through the air. With my powerful jaws, I'd give it a good, hearty toss, sending it on a majestic journey into the horizon.

Step 2: The Watch

Now, here comes the fun part. As my trusty ball flew through the air, I'd watch with intense focus.

My eyes locked onto it like a hawk spotting its prey. But here's the twist: I'd watch my owner, not the ball.

Step 3: The Retrieval

Once the ball touched down in a patch of tall grass, a bush, or even a puddle, my human would dutifully bound after it. No matter where that ball landed, I knew my owner would be there, plunging into hedges, trudging through mud, or parting tall grass like a champion explorer.

Step 4: The Joy

With the ball successfully retrieved, my owner would return, panting and perhaps a bit muddy. But here's the magic—when they handed the ball back to me, their face would light up with joy, and I'd wag my tail with all the enthusiasm a dog can muster.

Step 5: The Repeat

The cycle would begin anew, as I sent the ball on another adventure, and my owner would dash off to bring it back. It was a delightful game of fetch like no other.

Now, for the "Waggy Tailed Wisdom" I'd like to impart. Fetch is more than just a game; it's a beautiful exchange of love and joy between a dog and their human. It's not about how perfectly the ball is thrown or how precisely it's retrieved. It's about the shared moments of excitement, laughter, and boundless happiness.

So, my dear humans, remember that life's greatest treasures are often found in the most unconventional places. Embrace the unexpected, revel in the joy of the chase, and let your heart wag with the sheer delight of it all.

With boundless affection,

Cyril

CHAPTER 47

SQUIRREL-CHASING ADVENTURES WITH BOWIE THE SAUSAGE DOG

Panty, pant, pant, dear humans! I'm Bowie, the daring Dachshund, and I'm here to regale you with tales of my epic squirrel-chasing adventures and the profound love I have for those bushy-tailed critters.

You see, squirrels are more than just woodland creatures; they're my favourite playmates and, occasionally, my most worthy adversaries.

The Quest

It all begins when I spot one of those fluffy squirrel tails twitching in the distance. My heart quickens, and I can't resist the urge to give chase. It's not just about catching them; it's the thrill of the pursuit—the chase that ignites my tiny legs into action.

The Chase

I bound through the grass, zigzagging like a speed demon, following their erratic movements among the trees. They hop from branch to branch, and I dart beneath, hoping to outsmart them. It's a dance, a game of strategy, and I'm determined to win.

The Love

But here's the twist, my dear humans—I don't chase squirrels out of hatred. No, quite the opposite. I chase them because I adore them. Those little furry creatures with their cheeky personalities and acrobatic antics have captured my heart. It's not about catching them; it's about celebrating their existence.

Waggy Tailed Wisdom

And now, for some "Waggy Tailed Wisdom." Chasing squirrels reminds me that life is full of playful opportunities. It's not always about reaching a destination or achieving a goal. Sometimes, the journey itself is the greatest reward.

Just like squirrels, our lives are filled with moments of joy, excitement, and unexpected encounters. Embrace them, relish in the pursuit of your passions, and find delight in the simple act of chasing your dreams.

So, my dear humans, don't be afraid to chase your own "squirrels" with enthusiasm and determination. Whether it's a hobby, a dream, or a new adventure, remember that the thrill of the chase can be just as fulfilling as reaching the finish line.

With boundless squirrel-loving spirit,

Bowie

CHAPTER 48

WALKIES WONDERLAND - A WOLFHOUND'S TALE

Woof, my lovely humans! I'm Wander, the Wolfhound, and today I'm thrilled to share with you the exhilarating adventure that is "walkies" and the boundless excitement that builds up to it.

Each morning, as the sun peeks over the horizon, I can feel it in my bones—today is a "walkies" day. The mere mention of the word, the jingle of a leash, or the sight of my human's walking shoes fills me with anticipation. It's as if the universe itself conspires to bring us this moment.

Before we even step out the door, there's a ritual—a dance, you might say. My tail wags vigorously, creating a symphony of excitement. I perform my playful twirls, my ears perked up in joyful anticipation. We're not just going for a walk; we're embarking on a grand adventure!

And then, it happens. The door swings open, revealing a world of wonders. The scents of the outdoors greet me like old friends, and I'm ready to explore. My paws hit the pavement, and I'm off, with my human close behind.

Every walk is an odyssey, a journey of discovery. There are new paths to tread, fresh smells to savour, and fellow canine companions to meet along the way. Each blade of grass, every tree, and even the smallest pebble holds a secret waiting to be unravelled.

Now, let's talk about "Waggy Tailed Wisdom." The anticipation and excitement leading up to "walkies" remind us that life is full of precious moments waiting to be embraced. Whether it's a walk in the park, a new project, or an adventure yet to be embarked upon, the build-up is often as valuable as the destination itself.

My dear humans, relish the thrill of anticipation in your own lives. Find joy in the small moments of excitement that lead to the grand adventures. Remember that every day holds the promise of something wonderful, and it's up to you to embrace it with enthusiasm and an open heart.

With boundless anticipation,

Wander

CHAPTER 49

STARING AT MY HUMANS - A DOG'S JEDI MIND TRICK

Good day to you, dear humans! I'm Elie, your faithful English Setter, and I have a little secret I'd like to share with you. You see, we dogs have a Jedi mind trick of our own, and it involves something we do quite naturally—staring at you.

Now, you might be wondering why we do it and what we hope to achieve. Well, allow me to reveal the inner workings of this age-old canine art.

The Power of Connection: When I gaze deeply into your eyes, it's not just because I find you fascinating (which I do, by the way). It's a way for me to connect with you on a deeper level, to let you know that we share a special bond. In those moments, it's as if we're communicating without words, and it warms my furry heart.

Willing You to Play: You may have noticed that I often employ my Jedi mind trick when I'm feeling playful. I lock eyes with you, hoping that my intense stare will convey my desire for a game of fetch, a walk in the park, or some good old belly rubs. You see, humans sometimes need a gentle nudge to remember that playtime is essential.

Night-time Watchdog: At night, when you're asleep and the world is quiet, I can't help but keep an eye on you. My Jedi stare becomes a silent vigil, ensuring that you're safe and sound. I'm your loyal guardian, and my presence is a source of comfort.

Desire for Treats: Ah, treats! They hold a special place in my heart, and I've noticed that my persistent gaze tends to work wonders when I'm hoping for a tasty morsel. Sometimes, I simply can't resist using my Jedi mind trick to convince you that a treat would be a splendid idea.

Unconditional Love: Most importantly, when I stare at you, it's a way for me to express my unwavering love and devotion. Dogs have an incredible ability to convey their emotions through their eyes. It's my way of saying, "I adore you, and I'm grateful for the love you've showered upon me."

Now, for the Waggy Tailed Wisdom, my dear humans. Remember that when your furry friend stares at you, it's more than just a gaze—it's a heartfelt connection, a plea for interaction, and a declaration of love. Embrace these moments, for they are a testament to the extraordinary bond we share.

So, next time you catch your dog employing the Jedi mind trick of staring, go ahead and engage with them. Play a game, offer a treat, or simply return their loving gaze. For in those moments, you'll find the true magic of our canine-human relationship.

With love and a Jedi wink,

Elie

CHAPTER 50

THE ENCHANTING WORLD OF DEERS AND RABBITS - SOFIA'S PERSPECTIVE

Hello there, dear humans! I'm Sofia, the spirited Sproogle—a delightful mix of Springer Spaniel and Poodle. Today, I want to regale you with tales of two enchanting creatures I've had the pleasure of encountering—deer and rabbits. These furry friends hold a special place in my doggy heart, and I'd love to share their magic with you.

The Dance of the Deer:

Deers are like the elegant ballerinas of the forest, and they've become my favourite woodland companions. When I spot a deer gracefully gliding through the trees, my heart races with excitement. It's like a game of tag, but they don't know we're playing!

You see, deer have a unique way of capturing my attention. Their graceful leaps and bounding strides are a mesmerising spectacle. When they bound away, I can't help but chase after them, my paws pounding the earth with wild abandon. It's a game of chase that fills me with exhilaration.

But here's the magical part: I don't actually want to catch them. I just want to join in their dance, to be part of their world for a fleeting moment. So, if you ever see me darting through the woods with a sparkle in my eye, know that I'm sharing a secret waltz with my deer friends.

Romp with the Rabbits:

Now, let's talk about rabbits, the merry pranksters of the meadow. These small, fluffy creatures have an uncanny ability to make me giggle with delight. When I spot a rabbit darting among the tall grasses, I can't resist giving chase.

Rabbits are quick, but so am I! We engage in a merry game of hide-and-seek, zigzagging through the fields. It's a joyful pursuit, and their bunny hops are simply irresistible. There's something infectious about their boundless energy that fills me with happiness.

But here's the secret: I'm not really trying to catch them either. I just want to be part of their world, to share a laugh and a twirl in the grass. In those moments, it's as if we're all kids at heart, revelling in the sheer joy of being alive.

Waggy Tailed Wisdom... So, what can we learn from my enchanting adventures with deer and rabbits? Well, it's a reminder that life is meant to be lived with unbridled enthusiasm. Sometimes, we get so caught up in the busyness of our human world that we forget to dance, to play, and to revel in the simple pleasures.

Take a cue from moi, Sofia the Sproogle and embrace the magic around you. Find your own version of deer dances and rabbit romps, whether it's chasing your dreams, savouring nature's beauty, or simply sharing a joyful moment with loved ones.

In the company of deer and rabbits, I've discovered that life is a grand adventure, and every day is a chance to twirl in the meadow of possibilities. So, my dear humans, remember to chase your dreams, embrace your inner child, and live life with a heart full of wagging tails.

With boundless joy,

Sofia

CHAPTER 51

THE TWIRL BEFORE THE POOP - HARRY'S TALES

Hello, hellooooo dear humans! I'm Harry, the Havanese with a flair for the dramatic and a tale to tell about the curious canine ritual known as "The Twirl Before the Poop." Prepare to be entertained and enlightened!

The Grand Entrance:

Picture this: a serene morning stroll, the sun peeking over the horizon, and the world awakening to a new day. It's the perfect setting for my morning ritual. As I approach my chosen spot, I pause dramatically, surveying the area like a thespian on stage.

The Elegant Twirl:

Ah, the twirl! It's not just a random spin; it's a carefully choreographed ballet. I lift one delicate paw, then the other, twirling gracefully in a full circle, as if to say, "Ladies and gentlemen, prepare yourselves for the main event." It's all about building anticipation, you see.

The Artful Pose:

With the twirl complete, I strike a pose. I extend one hind leg with poise, creating a picturesque tableau. My head held high; my tail arched in perfect symmetry—every detail matters in this artistic performance.

The Poop, Finally:

And then, with a flourish, I assume the position. The audience (which often consists of curious squirrels and bewildered humans) watches in rapt attention as I finally do my business. It's a moment of relief, a climax to the exquisite build-up that came before.

Waggy Tailed Wisdom:

Now, you may wonder, why this elaborate dance before something as ordinary as pooping? Well, dear humans, it's a reminder that life is full of small rituals and moments that can be turned into something special. Embrace the whimsy, add flair to your daily routines, and find joy in the simplest of actions.

"The Twirl Before the Poop" is a testament to the idea that every moment, no matter how mundane, can be an opportunity to express yourself and bring a touch of theatre to your life. So, twirl, pose, and make your daily rituals a work of art. After all, life is your stage, and you are the star.

With a twirl and a woof,

Harry

CHAPTER 52

GAS AND GIGGLES - GEMIMA'S PERSPECTIVE

Woofy woof woof, dear humans! I'm Gemima, the guardian of grace and elegance, or so I like to think. You see, in the world of canine flatulence, I've had my fair share of embarrassing moments.

Now, let's talk about passing wind. It happens to the best of us, even the most poised and polished pups like me. Sometimes, it sneaks out when you least expect it, like during a royal tea party with fellow canines. The room suddenly falls silent, and all eyes turn to you in shock. Oh, the embarrassment!

But there are other times when it takes you by surprise, and you can't help but be horrified by the unexpected noise and odour. It's as if your body has betrayed you, and you're left wondering if it's time to hide in shame.

Yet, there's a curious side to it too. Sometimes, when I pass wind, I find myself turning around, sniffing the air as if I'm investigating a mysterious scent. It's as if my own gas is a puzzle I need to solve, a riddle of smells.

Soooo, let's discuss the 'Waggy Tailed Wisdom' I'd like to share. Passing wind, while often embarrassing, is a reminder that we're all creatures of nature, and there's humour even in our most embarrassing moments.

Life can throw surprises at us, just like those unexpected toots. And while we can't always control what happens, we can choose how we react. Instead of being horrified, we can embrace the humorous side of life, laugh at ourselves, and find joy in the little moments.

Well, my dear humans, the next time you're caught off guard by life's unexpected quirks, take a leaf out of my book. Embrace the gas and giggles and remember that laughter is the best response to any situation. After all, life is too short not to find joy in the unexpected.

With a twirl and a laugh,

Gemima

CHAPTER 53

THE ART OF WAGGING - TALES OF A LABRADOR'S TAIL

Hello, there, fellow humans and dog enthusiasts! I'm Locky, the Labrador, and I'm here to share the fascinating world of tail wagging with you.

Now, you might think that a tail is just a tail, but oh, the tales my tail can tell! You see, tail wagging is a language of its own, and I'm quite the fluent speaker. It's like I have a built-in mood indicator right there on my backside, ready to convey all my feelings.

First, there's the classic wag. It's friendly, it's welcoming, and it says, "Hey there, pal! Let's be friends!" I love using this one when I see my humans or meet new dogs at the park. It's like extending a virtual pawshake.

Then, there's the happy wag, where my entire hindquarters join in the dance. It's like I've got a little party going on back there. You know, when I've got my favorite squeaky toy or when my humans mention the magical word "walkies."

But let's not forget the supercharged wag, where I go into turbo mode, and my tail whizzes around so fast it's almost a blur. That's when I'm over the moon, and I might even take off like a helicopter if I'm not careful!

Now, here's the secret to the art of tail wagging: it's not just about the wag itself, but how you position it. I can wag to the left, to the right, or straight up in the air. It's like a secret code only us dogs understand. Left says, "I'm feeling friendly." Right says, "I'm not so sure about this," and up in the air says, "I'm the top dog around here!"

But here's the waggy-tailed wisdom for you humans: Learn to read the tails of the dogs you meet. It's like our way of saying hello, expressing joy, or even telling you when we're anxious. By understanding our tail language, you can connect with us on a deeper level and make us even happier pups.

So, next time you see a dog like me waggling our tails, remember that it's more than just a wiggle—it's a heartfelt conversation in canine. And when you return the gesture with a smile or a gentle scratch behind the ears, you've just made a furry friend for life!

Wagging my tail with delight,

Locky

CHAPTER 54

THE JOY OF HOWLING: A LAPPONIAN HERDER'S PERSPECTIVE

Wooooooooooooooo, dear humans! I'm Joana, the howling maestro, or so I like to think. You see, in the world of canine communication, howling is my forte, and it's a joyous symphony that's meant to be shared.

First, let's talk about the different types of howls. There's the soulful, moonlit serenade to the distant cousins—the wolves. This howl is full of longing and echoes through the quiet night, uniting me with the wild world beyond.

Then there's the neighbourhood howl-along, where I join the chorus of fellow canines. It's like a canine conference call where we discuss important matters like squirrel sightings and mail deliveries. It's a way of saying, "Hey, I'm here, and I'm part of this pack too!"

But let's not forget the joyous celebration howl. It's the one I save for special occasions like birthdays, holidays, or when my humans return home after a long day. This howl is filled with excitement and pure happiness.

Now, you might wonder, "Joana, why do you love to howl?" Well, let me share some waggy tailed wisdom with you:

Howling isn't just about making noise; it's about connecting with the world around me. It's a form of expression that transcends words. It's my way of celebrating life, expressing my emotions, and letting others know I'm here, a vital part of the pack.

So, my dear humans, take a page from my howling handbook. Celebrate the moments that matter, express your joys and sorrows, and, most importantly, connect with the world and those around you. Whether it's through laughter, song, or even a heartfelt howl, embrace the beauty of communication and connection.

With a joyful howl and a tail wag, woooooooooooooooooooooooooo!

Joana

CHAPTER 55

CANINE CULINARY CAPERS - A SALUKI'S PERSPECTIVE

Chew, chew, snuffle and chew, dear humans! I'm Silky, the Saluki, and today I'm here to regale you with tales of canine culinary delights, quirks, and adventures.

Okie dokie, let's talk about the diverse ways we dogs approach our meals. Some of us are connoisseurs, savouring every bite as if it were a gourmet delicacy. Others, well, we're more like enthusiastic foodies, ready to raid picnics and snuffle anything that smells remotely edible.

In my circle of furry friends, there's quite the range of culinary preferences. Take my buddies, Max and Luna, for instance. They're the adventurous types, always ready for a picnic raid. Whether it's sausages, sandwiches, or even a bag of chips, they'll snatch it up with glee. The thrill of the chase and the taste of the forbidden make it all the more exciting.

On the other paw, there's little Oliver, my puppy playmate. He's the epitome of picky eating. Chicken? He'll turn his nose up at it. Sausages? No, thank you. He's got gourmet tastes and won't settle for anything less than his specially prepared, top-quality kibble. It's a mystery to me, but to each dog their own, I suppose.

Now, for some 'Waggy Tailed Wisdom' on this matter. Food is one of life's simple pleasures, whether you're a foodie like Max and Luna or a discerning diner like Oliver. It teaches us that diversity is the spice of life, even when it comes to our meals.

So, my dear humans, as you enjoy your own culinary adventures, remember to savour the flavours, embrace the occasional indulgence, and appreciate the unique tastes and preferences that make life all the more delicious. After all, a shared meal with your furry friend is a moment of pure joy and connection.

Bon appétit!

Silky

CHAPTER 56

SNOOZING IN UNUSUAL POSITIONS - A DOG'S PERSPECTIVE

Snore, sigh, snore, huff, dear humans! I'm Buster, your friendly neighbourhood Briard, and I'm here to regale you with tales of my extraordinary napping adventures. You see, there's nothing quite like a good nap, and I've taken this art form to new heights—literally!

First, let's talk about nap locations. Oh, the possibilities are endless! While some may prefer the cosy confines of a doggy bed, I'm known to be a bit of an adventurer when it comes to my siestas. You'll often find me under desks, burrowed into dens, or even claiming the comfiest spot on your sofa when you're not looking. But the real magic happens when I nap in the most unexpected places.

You see, I've mastered the art of doggy levitation. Yes, you heard that right! I can transform your ordinary armchair into a plush, cloud-like bed with just a flick of my tail. It's all in the tail's secret technique, you know. By curling it just so, I create a cocoon of comfort that cradles me in dreamy slumber.

Now, let's talk about my penchant for snoozing in unusual positions. I'm sure you've seen dogs stretched out on their backs, legs akimbo, in what looks like an acrobatic display. But my friends, that's just the tip of the nap-time iceberg. I've been known to contort myself into shapes that would make a yoga master jealous.

From twisted pretzels to gravity-defying poses, I find the quirkiest positions to snooze in. It's like a daily doggy yoga session, and trust me, it keeps me limber and ready for my next adventure. And who doesn't love waking up to see their Briard mastering the art of the "upside-down, inside-out" nap?

Now, for some Waggy Tailed Wisdom I'd like to impart to you humans. Napping isn't just about resting our bodies; it's about finding comfort and joy in the simplest of moments. Embrace the whimsy of life, like a Briard's contorted nap, and relish the unique beauty in unexpected places. Take time to rest, rejuvenate, and discover your own delightful, gravity-defying moments of bliss.

So, my dear friends, whether you're napping in your office chair or snoozing like a Briard pretzel, remember that life's quirks and comforts are meant to be celebrated. Embrace them, cherish them, and nap like there's no gravity to hold you down!

With a tail that's always ready for a wag,

Buster

CHAPTER 57

DOGGY KISSES AND NUZZLES - A LOVE LANGUAGE BY MISSY THE AKITA

Hello, dear humans! I'm Missy, your friendly neighbourhood Akita, and I'm here to share a little secret with you. You see, in the enchanting realm of doggy love, there's no gesture quite as heart-warming as a tender kiss or a gentle nuzzle.

Picture this: a sunny afternoon, the scent of freshly cut grass in the air, and you, my cherished human, sitting on the porch after a long day. That's the perfect moment for a good old-fashioned doggy smooch.

When it comes to kisses, we Akitas are masters of affection. Our soft, warm tongues can convey a thousand emotions with a single lick. It's how we express our love, gratitude, and happiness. It's our way of saying, "You mean the world to me."

But there's more to it than that. You see, when we nuzzle or plant a wet one on your face, it's our way of bonding with you. It's an intimate moment where we bridge the gap between species and connect on a profound level. In those shared seconds, we communicate without words, letting you know that we're here for you, through thick and thin.

Now, I'll let you in on a little secret. The occasional nose-lick isn't just about love; it's about curiosity too. We want to know where you've been, who you've met, and what adventures you've had. So, when we aim for your nostrils, it's our way of saying, "Tell me everything, dear human!"

But here's the twist: as much as we adore giving kisses, we cherish receiving them just as much. It's a two-way street, my friends. So, the next time we pucker up and offer you our slobbery affections, don't be shy. Lean in and share the love. After all, the world could use a bit more unconditional love and a lot more slobbery smooches.

And now, for some waggy tailed wisdom: In a world that sometimes feels too busy and serious, don't underestimate the power of a simple kiss or a loving nuzzle. It's a reminder that love transcends language and boundaries. Embrace those moments of connection, be it with a furry friend or a fellow human and let your heart soar with joy. Bark, wag, love – it's the sweetest language of all.

With love and wet-nosed kisses,

Missy

CHAPTER 58

BEING A GOOD BOY AND A GOOD GIRL - LESSONS IN PRAISE AND JOY

Woof, dear humans! I'm Archibald, the Airedale, and this is my tale of being a good boy. You see, it's not just about fetching sticks or sitting on command; it's about the pure delight of praise.

Archibald's Perspective:

Being a good boy means wagging my tail with pride when I follow the rules. I sit when asked, fetch with enthusiasm, and even lend a helping paw when my humans need it. But the real joy? Oh, it's in the praise they shower upon me.

When my humans say, "Good boy, Archie!" I can feel the love and pride in their voices. It's like music to my floppy ears. The warmth in their eyes and the pats on my head tell me that I'm their hero, their loyal companion. That feeling is better than any treat or toy.

Annie's Perspective:

Hi there, I'm Annie, Archibald's sister. Being a good girl is my specialty. I sit pretty, offer my paw for a shake, and stay when told. The treats that follow are delightful, but it's the praise that makes my heart sing.

When my humans say, "Good girl, Annie!" I know I've done something wonderful. It's as if I've painted a masterpiece with my good behaviour, and they are my enthusiastic audience. Their smiles and cuddles are my biggest rewards.

Waggy Tailed Wisdom: Now, dear humans, let us impart some waggy tailed wisdom to you. Praise is a magical thing. It's more than just words; it's a celebration of the bond between us. When you praise us, you fill our hearts with joy and encouragement.

So, whether we're being good boys or good girls, or simply being ourselves, remember that a kind word, a loving touch, or a genuine "well done" can make our tails wag and our hearts burst with happiness. Your praise is the greatest treat you can give us, and it strengthens the beautiful connection we share.

Embrace the joy of celebrating the goodness in each other. Just like Archibald and me, find moments to praise and be praised, for it brings warmth and light to every day.

With love and tail wags,

Archibald & Annie

CHAPTER 59

UNCONDITIONAL LOVE - A TERRIER'S PERSPECTIVE

Love, love, love!!! Dear humans! I'm Asta, your friendly neighborhood American Hairless Terrier, and I'm here to delve into the deep and ethereal concept of unconditional love. You see, we dogs have an innate understanding of this extraordinary force, and I'd love to share some insights with you.

Unconditional love, to me, is like the gentle caress of a breeze on a warm, sunny day—a feeling so pure and comforting that it transcends words. It's the bond that forms between us dogs and our beloved humans, a connection that goes beyond the surface and delves into the very essence of our souls.

As an American Hairless Terrier, I may look a bit different from other dogs with my smooth, hairless coat, but beneath this unique exterior beats a heart filled with boundless love. I don't judge based on appearances, and I certainly don't hold grudges. My love flows freely and without conditions, embracing you with every wag of my tail.

You see, I've learned that unconditional love is about acceptance. It's about cherishing every moment we share, regardless of the circumstances. It's the joy of bounding to the door to greet you, whether you've had a good day or a challenging one. It's the comfort I offer when you're feeling low, my warm presence a soothing balm for your soul.

Unconditional love knows no bounds, no limits. It's patient and forgiving, teaching us that mistakes are merely opportunities to grow closer. I've witnessed how a gentle touch, a kind word, or a shared adventure can strengthen the unbreakable bond between a dog and their human.

Now, for some Waggy Tailed Wisdom I'd like to share with you. Unconditional love, as I've come to understand it, is a treasure that enriches our lives. Embrace it fully, both in your relationships with us dogs and with your fellow humans. Cherish the moments of pure connection, where love knows no conditions or judgments.

In a world that can sometimes feel divided, let unconditional love be your guiding light. Extend kindness, forgiveness, and acceptance to others, just as we dogs do with open hearts. Remember that love, in its truest form, has the power to heal, unite, and elevate the human spirit.

So, my dear friends, may you experience the ethereal beauty of unconditional love in all its glory. And may you be inspired to share this boundless love with the world, creating a brighter and more compassionate tomorrow.

With a heart that knows no conditions,

Asta

CHAPTER 60

DOGGY DIVAS AND MASTER MANIPULATORS - A CANINE PERSPECTIVE

Darling humans, I am Beatrice, the epitome of canine sophistication, or so I like to think. You see, in the world of doggy divas and master manipulators, I have quite the flair for the dramatic.

To begin with, let's talk about manipulation. Oh, the art of getting exactly what you want without lifting a paw! Whether it's those irresistible treats or a spot on the comfiest sofa, we dogs have mastered the subtle tactics to make our humans bend to our will. I, for one, have a patented puppy-dog stare that can melt even the coldest of hearts.

But here's where the humour comes in. Sometimes, in our enthusiasm to be the centre of attention, we doggy divas and master manipulators can get carried away. I've been known to deploy my charm and then promptly knock over a vase or sneakily nab a sandwich from the kitchen counter. Oh, the scandal! It's a reminder that even the most refined of canines can have their moments of mischief.

Now, let's discuss the 'Waggy Tailed Wisdom' I'd like to impart. Doggy divas and master manipulators have an important lesson for humans. Life should be enjoyed to the fullest, with all its quirks and whims. Don't be afraid to express your desires, chase your dreams, and, yes, indulge in a treat or two.

But also remember that true charm lies in kindness and empathy. Use your powers of persuasion for good, like spreading love and joy to those around you. After all, isn't that what truly makes life delightful?

So, my dear humans, channel your inner Beatrice and approach each day with confidence, charm, and a generous dose of compassion. And remember, the world is your stage, so shine brightly and share the love.

With a paw wave and a twinkle in my eye,

Beatrice

CHAPTER 61

THE BEST THINGS ABOUT BEING A DOG

1. Unconditional Love: Dogs love their humans with unwavering devotion. They teach us the beauty of loving without judgment or conditions, just like Asta, the American Hairless Terrier.

2. Pure Joy in the Little Things: Dogs find immense joy in the simplest pleasures, whether it's chasing a ball, rolling in the mud like Mildred the Mudi, or wagging their tails at the sight of their favorite human.

3. Living in the Present: Dogs live in the moment, savouring each experience as it comes. They remind us to be present, just like Wander the Wolfhound on his daily walkies.

4. Playfulness: Dogs are experts in play, whether it's fetching a ball like Harry the Havapoo or chasing squirrels like Bowie the Sproogle. They teach us to embrace our inner child and find fun in everyday life.

5. Sharing Love and Affection: Dogs like Lois the Lhasa Apso are masters of affection, reminding us to express our love openly and without reservation.

6. Exploration and Curiosity: Dogs, like Sofia the Sproogle, remind us of the joy of exploration and discovery, even if it's just chasing rabbits or deer in the yard.

7. Friendship and Camaraderie: Dogs understand the value of friendship, as seen in Darryl's pack of rescue dogs from various corners of the world.

8. Adaptability and Resilience: Dogs like Sheila the Shi Tzu teach us about resilience, especially during their puppy chewing phase. They adapt to new circumstances with a wagging tail.

9. Pure Happiness in a Tum Tum Rub: Rufus the multi-Cocka-poo Shih-Tzu shows us that true contentment can be found in a simple belly rub.

10. The Healing Power of Laughter: Dogs, like Chuck and Daisy, engage in hilarious antics that make us laugh. They remind us that laughter is the best medicine.

Waggy-Tailed Wisdom for Humans:

1. Love Unconditionally: Embrace the practice of loving others without conditions or judgments, just as Asta does.

2. Savour the Small Joys: Find happiness in life's little moments, whether it's a sunny day or a warm cup of coffee. Follow the lead of joyful dogs like Sky, Porsha, and Chuck.

3. Live in the Present: Make an effort to be fully present in each moment, just as Wander does on his walks.

4. Embrace Playfulness: Make time for play and fun in your life, just as Harry, Bowie, and Lois do.

5. Express Affection: Don't hold back when it comes to expressing your love and affection for others, as demonstrated by Lois.

6. Stay Curious: Cultivate your curiosity and explore new things, just as Sofia does when chasing rabbits.

7. Value Friendship: Cherish your friendships and connect with others, like Darryl's diverse pack of rescue dogs.

8. Adapt and Bounce Back: When life throws you a curveball, remember the resilience of dogs like Sheila.

9. Find Contentment in Simple Pleasures: Enjoy the soothing comfort of simple pleasures, like a good tum tum rub.

10. Laughter is Healing: Don't forget to laugh, just as Chuck and Daisy bring humour to their lives.

These lessons from our furry friends can lead to a happier, more fulfilled life, filled with love, joy, and the wisdom of wagging tails.

WAGGY TAILED WISDOM

In a world of fur and floppy ears,
Where joy is bound to wagging rears,
Our canine pals have tales to tell,
With waggy wisdom, oh so swell!

When skies are grey and moods are low,
A pup's wagging tail will help you glow.
For in their wags, they softly say,
"Life's too short, so let's play today!"

They teach us love, no strings attached,
With cuddles, licks, and paws outstretched.
Their eyes gleam bright, like twinkling stars,
Reminding us that love knows no bars.

Each muddy puddle, each playful chase,
Is a lesson learned in their embrace.
With every bark and joyful leap,
In their wisdom, secrets they keep.

From sunrise walks to tum tum rubs,
They show us life's most precious hubs.
In sniffing flowers and rolling in muck,
They say, "Hey, friend, don't pass the luck!"

When troubles brew and times get tough,
Their loyalty is more than enough.
They nuzzle close, with hearts so pure,
Their presence, a love that will endure.

So, heed the waggy tailed decree,
Live life with zest and wild, carefree.
In wagging tails and joyful barks,
We find the wisdom in their sparks.

For in their world of fur and fun,
They teach us all how it's well done.
With waggy tails and wisdom shared,
With our canine friends, we're doubly paired.

So, when life feels like a stormy sea,
Remember waggy tailed philosophy.
Live, love, laugh, and don't delay,
With waggy wisdom, seize the day!

Woof!
If you have enjoyed this, then please share this
with your pack and even review it if you have time
to 'paws and reflect'

Lots of love
Rufus
&
Ruby

Printed in Great Britain
by Amazon